"*The Wounded Angel* considers the uses of so-called secular literature to convey illuminations of mystery, the unsayable, the hidden otherness, the Holy One. Saint Ignatius urged us to find God in all things, and Paul Lakeland demonstrates how that's theologically possible in fictions whose authors had no spiritual or religious intentions. A fine and much-needed reflection."

— Ron Hansen
Santa Clara University

"Renowned ecclesiologist Paul Lakeland explores in depth one of his earliest but perduring interests: the impact of reading serious modern fiction. He convincingly argues for an inner link between faith and religious imagination. Drawing on a copious cross section of thoughtful novels (not all of them 'edifying'), he reasons that the joy of reading is more than entertainment but rather potentially salvific transformation of our capacity to love and be loved. Art may accomplish what religion does not always achieve. The numerous titles discussed here belong on one's must-read list!"

— Michael A. Fahey, SJ
Fairfield University

"Paul Lakeland claims that 'the work of the creative artist is always somehow bumping against the transcendent.' What a lovely thought and what a perfect summary of the subtle and significant argument made in *The Wounded Angel*. Gracefully moving between theology and literature, religious content and narrative form, Lakeland reminds us both of how imaginative faith is and of how imbued with mystery and grace literature is. Lakeland's range of interests—Coleridge and Louise Penny, Marilynne Robinson and Shusaku Endo—is wide, and his ability to trace connections between these texts and relate them to large-scale theological questions is impressive. This is an essential read for those interested in the relationship between the religious and literary imaginations."

— Anthony Domestico
Assistant Professor of Literature
Purchase College, SUNY

The Wounded Angel

Fiction and the Religious Imagination

Paul Lakeland

LITURGICAL PRESS

Collegeville, Minnesota

www.litpress.org

Cover design by Ann Blattner. *The Wounded Angel* by Hugo Simberg (1873–1917). Image courtesy of Wikimedia Commons.

1	2	3	4	5	6	7	8	9

Library of Congress Cataloging-in-Publication Data

Names: Lakeland, Paul, 1946– author.
Title: The wounded angel : fiction and the religious imagination / Paul
 Lakeland.
Description: Collegeville, Minnesota : Liturgical Press, 2017.
Identifiers: LCCN 2016045751 (print) | LCCN 2017005771 (ebook) |
 ISBN 9780814646229 | ISBN 9780814646472 (ebook)
Subjects: LCSH: Fiction—Religious aspects—Christianity. | Religion
 and literature.
Classification: LCC PN3351 .L35 2017 (print) | LCC PN3351 (ebook) |
 DDC 809.3/9382—dc23
LC record available at https://lccn.loc.gov/2016045751

Contents

Introduction

"All art of the highest order is religious in essence."
(Simone Weil)

"Every truly great work of art orients you to what isn't there,
what can't be seen or described or named."
(Martin Scorsese)

"I'm certain that the only meanings that are worth anything in a
work of art are those that the artist himself knows nothing about."
(Virginia Woolf)

In the last ten years or so of the thirty-five years I have been
teaching theology I have increasingly turned to works of fiction
in order to focus the attention of undergraduates, who much
as they often resist reading are certainly more comfortable with
a novel than a theological treatise. At times I have wondered
if all I am doing here is what Mark Edmundson does with
literature, when he says that "humanism is the belief that it is
possible for some of us, and maybe more than some, to use
secular writing as the preeminent means for shaping our
lives."[1] But then he did also say that "the most consequential
questions for an individual life . . . are related to questions of
faith."[2] So I have turned the question around, to ask if in fact
there is much difference at all between the struggle to shape

[1] Mark Edmundson, *Why Read?* (New York: Bloomsbury, 2005), 86.
[2] Ibid., 27.

viii   *The Wounded Angel*

one's life and the struggle to believe. For a person with a fully formed faith, there is no question but that it shapes the believer's life, maybe that it *is* the shape of that life, though not in a way that all growth is over and everything is closed. Faith can grow richer, and it can die. Not everyone has been gifted with this kind of faith, however, and in our day lots of people are persuaded that they would not want it, even if they are not really aware of what the "it" is. Both of these kinds of people have been present in my classes and they are in all of our lives. So in what ways might fiction be an appropriate conduit of information and inspiration in the task of being more and more fully human? How, indeed, can fiction aid faith, and—equally important—how can the elements of transcendence that lie behind the greatest fiction influence the secular reader?

During the same ten or so years I have also written four books on different aspects of the Second Vatican Council and its relationship to the role of laypeople in the church. This present book takes a very different direction, but there are two important theological takeaways from the work of the council that to a high degree inform and to some extent motivate the work of these pages. In the first place, Vatican II affirmed the ubiquity of divine grace. God is at work everywhere in the world, and while the church has a particular role to play it has no monopoly on grace. Second, following this understanding of divine grace and taking it in a slightly more radical direction, section 44 of the Pastoral Constitution on the Church in the Modern World, *Gaudium et Spes*, was at pains to point out that while the church has much to offer the secular world, it also has much to learn from it. So while there will be no further reference to the council and no more quotations from its documents, the conviction that church and world dialogue on a level playing field in the light of grace suffuses everything that follows here.

There are two supporting roles for literature to play in people's lives: one directed more toward those for whom the act of faith already shapes their lives, and one for those for whom it is not or not yet real.[3] The work of the creative artist is always somehow bumping up against transcendence, hinting at the unsayable even in the process of saying something quite definite or important that is not itself the transcendent. For the person of faith, then, fiction offers a wider perspective on the scope of grace by telling a story that integrates grace *and* sin in a way that defeats simplistic oppositions between the two. No person of faith doubts that we are all both graced and sinful, but grace and sin are so often held apart, while fiction may insist that they are present not only in the same person but perhaps even in the same act. The complex attractiveness of great fiction to the person of faith (or is it seen by some as a threat?) is that it makes it impossible to separate out sin and grace. For the person who does not possess faith in the narrow sense, fiction of course presents the same mix of sin and grace, but now in a way that makes it possible for this person to begin to see that in accepting the very fusion of sin and grace in individuals and communities there is a statement being made about loving acceptance that does not make sense in our ordinary categories and which therefore offers the invitation to look beyond simply what-is. To the person of faith, fiction supports love of the world as it is and contradicts the simplistic separation of the sacred and the profane. To the

---

[3] I have struggled with the terminology here. On the one hand, I do want to distinguish between people who would claim some kind of religious faith and those who professedly do not, but as a Catholic theologian I work with the conviction that God's saving grace is at work in all people of whatever religious, spiritual, or plainly secular starting point. I also do not want to suggest that "secular" people are entirely without something that even they might recognize as a kind of faith. As Nietzsche's Zarathustra said, "Be faithful to the earth!" Moreover, the term "people of faith," which I use a great deal in what follows, lets atheists be atheists but is not always adequate to the variations among people of faith. So at times I will introduce the word "Christian" and occasionally "Catholic" to make my point more precisely. In the context, all of this will hopefully be clear.

x   *The Wounded Angel*

searcher or the agnostic, fiction teases with intimations of a beyond that may be either unnerving or intriguing but cannot be ignored.

If we understand fiction in this way, then we should be able to articulate a theology of literature, in particular a theology of fiction. This will most certainly not mean that we will be singling out professedly theological novels or those written by people of faith, still less novels that have either an open or hidden agenda to make a point about religion. The kinds of works that will claim our attention, as we will see at length in what follows, are those that independently of their authors' purposes or their subject matter bring the reader into an interpretive space where he or she is creatively engaged with transcendence, by whatever name. Religious reflection on the ways in which fiction brings the reader to an encounter with transcendence is itself a theology of literature. The fictions that we entertain may be stories of heroism or of evil, of greed or of self-denial, of love or of hatred, but it is what they inspire in the reader, not what they contain in themselves, that makes them fodder for religious reflection.

The Wounded Angel, which provides the title and the cover illustration of the book, is a fairly well-known and somewhat mysterious picture painted by the Finnish artist Hugo Simberg in 1903. Originally Simberg left the picture untitled, and although he eventually gave it its present name, he always studiously resisted offering any explanation of its components. Indeed, he insisted that it was to be interpreted as each viewer thought best, which allows for anyone to classify it as "just a picture of two boys in some kind of public park carrying an angel on a stretcher," or alternatively to dismiss it as "needlessly obscure." No doubt, there have been some viewers who have come to one or the other conclusion, but over the century since it was painted the consensus has been that there is more to it than just what you see, though what that "more" is will not be easy to pin down. Nor, given Simberg's instructions, will we be tempted to go looking for "the painter's intentions." If he had any, he is not telling. For this reason at least, *The Wounded Angel* offers us a fine opportunity to test how attentiveness to the text, for the painting is a text, allows each of us to interpret it to our own satisfaction and so to recognize the existence of the "more" or the mystery to which Martin Scorsese alludes in the quotation at the head of this introduction.

Hugo Simberg's painting hints at many of the issues we shall be considering. In the first place it points to my sense that faith and everyday life in today's world suffer alike from the impoverishment of the imagination. *Why* our imaginations are diminished is not the subject of this book, but *that* they are seems to me unassailable. The angel can certainly be understood as an icon of religious faith, and the wound as the product of our failure to imagine. The angel falls to earth because we fail to buoy it up on our faith, and the accusatory glance of the boy who takes up the rear is evidence enough that we are the ones under judgment. One of the reasons that religion in the West is under strain is that it is so much busier trying to retain the past than it is to embrace the present and look to the future. One of the consequences of the way we live now is that there is little time and seemingly equally little taste for attention to the works of the imagination, or for that matter for the challenging discipline of spiritual practices. Movies and television are preferred to literary fiction, and fiction to poetry. In an age of sound bites and short attention spans, both prayer and literary appreciation are luxuries that the majority of people seem to feel they can live without. But we do so at our peril, because somehow they threaten our sense of self. This is the wounded angel of our imaginations that, I believe, fiction can go a long way to healing.

There are several steps in the elaboration of this theology of fiction. First of all, we need to develop a more nuanced understanding of what is happening in the act of faith than we might usually employ. Part 1 of the book has three chapters, the first two exploring the idea of the act of faith from the medieval argument between Aquinas and Ockham through neo-scholastic and neo-Thomist efforts to reexpress it, to the theories of the imagination in Romantic literature, to more recent twentieth-century formulations of what is involved in the act of faith. These chapters are the most technically theological in the book, and those who are either uninterested in or allergic to the history of theology will probably skip over them or skim them. The important thing to grasp is that the history of the understanding of religious faith is one in which the relationship of the intellect and the imagination has been much debated and that in the end the priority is given to the imagination, without rejecting an intellectual component. When we come to see that the imagination plays a central role, the way is cleared to compare the process to that which takes place in the act of reading, and this is the subject of chapter 3. There is structural isomorphism between the two acts and substantive similarity in the way in which each reaches out to a beyond or an ultimate that is not ever fully accessible. While some of this chapter probably contains more literary theory than some readers will want, it is a critical chapter for establishing the basic thesis of the book, that the act of faith and the act of reading fiction have much in common structurally and have much to contribute to one another substantively.

The three chapters of part 2 explore in more detail some specific relationships between fiction and faith. In chapter 4 we begin from the reflections of Nathan Scott Jr. on literature and transcendence and then raise some questions about the contemporary impoverishment of the imagination, both religious and secular, before turning to an analysis of Albert Camus's novel *The Plague* to give more concreteness to what has thus far been somewhat abstract. Chapter 5 takes up the question of just how a novel that sets out to avoid "deep questions" can nevertheless succeed in raising them. Here we go from examining James Wood's theories on the demise of the sacred in modern fiction to a close look at Virginia Woolf's *To the Lighthouse* as, in some sense, a refutation of the idea that transcendence can be sidelined entirely, even in a simple stream of consciousness. Finally in this section, chapter 6 revolves around the challenging question of what it means to talk about Catholic novels or a Catholic sensibility in literature, wondering in particular if the changing shape of religious belonging makes the category less than helpful today.

In the third and final part of the book we address directly a theology of literature. We begin in chapter 7 by turning to a more extended consideration of Hugo Simberg's painting, *The Wounded Angel*, which can help us to think more clearly about the question of the interconnections of the religious and the secular as well as the tensions that exist between them. This tensive relationship is examined in two novels, Jim Harrison's *The Big Seven* and Flannery O'Connor's *Wise Blood*. Chapter 8 looks at how modern literature complicates our notions of holiness. We trace this first through a brief comparison of Graham Greene's *The Power and the Glory* and Shusaku Endo's riff on similar issues in *Silence*. We then stretch our understanding of where we might find holiness by exploring *Bailey's Café* by Gloria Naylor and the detective fiction of the Canadian author Louise Penny, whose mysterious world of Three Pines provides a textbook example of a community of sin and grace. Finally, in chapter 9 we turn to the question of how the substance of a fiction relates to the substance of faith. In the previous chapters our attention has principally been on the formal relationship between faith and fiction, but now we conclude by asking about how the plot of fiction relates to the plot of our own lives. For a Christian, the plot of the individual's life is somehow informed by the "plot" contained in the whole history of salvation or maybe more commonly in the plot of the life of Jesus, the paschal mystery of death and new life. We argue that fiction and life alike exhibit tensions between different understandings of happiness. There is the hedonistic search for the satisfaction of desires, and there is eudaemonism, the conviction that true happiness has more to do with being more and more fully who I am. And we bring the chapter and the book to a conclusion by illustrating this claim in three contemporary novels that represent in turn a more religious sensibility, a spiritual but not explicitly religious orientation, and a plainly secular character. If the argument works it will enlighten nonbelievers about the substance of lives of faith beyond dogma and narrowly religious rhetoric. And it will alert people of faith to their own tendencies toward imagining the scope of divine grace to be something much more constricted than in fact it is. Faith and fiction alike deal with a greater mystery than either fully appreciates, and each has much more in common with the other than it suspects.

❖ ❖ ❖

As always there are many institutions and individuals to thank for their assistance in various forms. First place must go to Fairfield University for the granting of a sabbatical leave and for the Robert Wall Award, both of which together enabled me to take a whole year off from teaching in order to work on this book. Second, I have to thank Michelle Ross and Mary Crimmins, who have kept the Center for Catholic Studies running as smoothly as ever, despite my much more erratic presence. Fr. Michael Fahey, SJ, scholar-in-residence at Fairfield University, read the whole manuscript carefully and made many invaluable suggestions, accompanied by equally important enthusiastic encouragement. Dr. John Slotemaker gave me invaluable help with some of the niceties of medieval thought, though the errors that remain are my own. James Crampsey, my Scottish Jesuit friend of half a century, deserves the credit for listening to my early meanderings about the proposed book and suggesting the painting of the wounded angel as something that might be helpful to me. Evidently, Jim, it was! My longtime friend and wonderful colleague, Dr. John

Thiel, has also read much of the text and, as always, has been unstinting in his careful attention to the argument, even when he might suspect that I would not have been pleased to hear all of what he had to say. We have shared work between ourselves for thirty-five years now, and I venture to say that neither of us has been the worse for it; I have certainly benefited enormously. This time around I am especially grateful for his urgings about the content of the final chapter. Portions of the manuscript have also been the subject of collegial discussions, with my colleagues in the Religious Studies Department at Fairfield, with the New Haven Theological Discussion Group, and with the members of the New York Area Workgroup for Constructive Theology. I am indebted to these groups for equal measure of thoughtful reading and consummate patience. My students in two courses I have taught off and on over the past decade, "Saints and Sinners" and "Belief and Unbelief," have helped me think through much of this material, even when they didn't know that was what they were doing. Hans Christoffersen at Liturgical Press has been his usual patient and affirming self. Amy Ambrosio, the mother of a former student, gave me a huge amount of help thinking about the old TV series *Northern Exposure*, and the fact that in the end I wrote little about it and will have disappointed her does not mean that I did not appreciate her insights. Beth Palmer, my wife and best friend, has left me to it for the most part but suffered through long efforts at clarification of thought on our frequent afternoon walks. And finally, since this may conceivably be the last book I will complete as a full-time teacher at Fairfield University, I want to record my appreciation for the community of teachers and scholars with whom I have had the privilege to work, laugh, and occasionally cry over these many years. They have been the most generous of colleagues, and I couldn't have done what I have done without them. Though, of course, the errors and weaknesses are entirely of my own creation.

Part One

The Act of Faith and the Act of Reading

Chapter One

What Is the Act of Faith?

Aquinas, Ockham, and A. J. Ayer:
What Counts as Evidence?

Let us begin with a little imaginative exercise. We are going to eavesdrop on a conversation taking place in a quiet and little-frequented corner of heaven, where there is a room that contains every creature comfort that a medieval mind could imagine. Of course it does, because this is heaven, though it is heaven as it could be imagined in the thirteenth and fourteenth centuries. No iPads, no memory foam. Beautifully carved but distinctly un-upholstered chairs sit around a solid oak table. Because this is heaven the daytime temperature is a steady 22 degrees Celsius (God, like most of the human race, eschews Fahrenheit). Which is just as well, since window glass wasn't invented for several more centuries, and the stretched animal skins that served to cover windows by the end of the four-teenth century kept out most of the light as well as the draft. There are two men sitting together in this room, one of them sufficiently well-upholstered himself that the absence of cush-ioning on the chairs is a matter of no moment. This is Thomas Aquinas (1225–1276), and his conversation partner is the much skinnier Englishman, William of Ockham (1280–1348). They could meet only in heaven because Ockham was born four years after Aquinas died. They speak in Latin, the language of the learned, but we will imagine them using Ockham's own tongue in its modern form since the English he spoke, when he spoke it, would be barely comprehensible to us today. Let us listen in for a few minutes.

Aquinas: *I wanted to get us together, William, because from our vantage point in eternity we can see only too well what kind of a mess subsequent history has made of our philosophical and theological writings. I am quite horrified when I look at my own treatment at the hands of those whom I thought were my follow-ers and who clearly thought they were saying what I had said— though perhaps they were actually saying what they wished I had said. Or even saying what they thought themselves and using my authority, such as it is, to authorize their strange conclusions.*

Ockham: *A good idea, Thomas. I cannot tell you how upset I am by the way in which my work was taken over by nominalists and eventually resulted in that terrible fiasco produced in the mid-twentieth century by Alfred Ayer, an Oxford scholar, God help us, and an arrant atheist. How the old place has gone to the dogs!*

Aquinas: *Take this question of the knowledge of God and how it is involved in the act of faith. I have never argued that human reason can know much about God, only that it can be predisposed to receive divine revelation by arriving, through observation and logic, at a sense that God exists and that God must have certain perfections to be God. Faith does not lie in the intellect, but there must be something in the intellect if the will is going to be able to lead the intellect to accept God.*

Ockham: *Well, of course, but if I may say so, your subsequent inter-preters can be excused to a degree for making this mistake because you do indeed insist that the intellect receives the data of faith as genuine evidence about God. I have never been able to see revelation as evidence, because evidence comes from intellectual activity, and there is no human intellectual activity in revelation. This is God's self-revelation, and all we can know truly about God comes from revelation, not from human reason.*

Aquinas: *Yes, but that's not quite the problem. The question of whether our knowledge of God comes from revelation is not at issue. My thoughts about natural knowledge of God are fragile and, frankly, not extensive. No, the true question is whether the divine revelation has the status of evidence. I think it does, and I know you disagree. Which may indeed be why your thinking ended up in logical positivism. How far is it from your view that there are only three ways in which we can attain knowledge of anything—that it must be "self-evident or known by experience or proved by the authority of Sacred Scripture"—to Ayer's position that only statements whose truth can be verified have any meaning, and so empirically unverifiable statements, which include ethical, metaphysical, and religious claims, are simply meaningless? Your inclusion of Scripture, which Ayer would obviously reject, seems to leave you open to being charged simultaneously with positivism and fideism. The first is a mistake and the second is a heresy.*

Ockham: *You know well enough that this is not my position. All I wish to claim is that the knowledge of God derived from divine revelation (a) is the only knowledge of God we can have and (b) does not qualify as knowledge in the normal human sense of the term because we have no evidence, other than the authority of revelation itself. So perhaps we are not so far apart as history has judged us to be.*

This imaginary exchange brings us right into the heart of the question about faith. In order to be able to believe, do we have to have some idea of God's existence before belief is possible, or is this kind of "natural knowledge of God" simply impossible? Can the human reason unaided by revelation arrive at any knowledge at all of God? The affirmative response to this question is usually classified as "natural theology," that is, theology that stands outside the knowledge that revelation provides to the person of faith. Its classic exposition is in Aquinas's work, and the best example can be found in his relatively well-known arguments for the existence of God. In each, human reason unaided by revelation can conclude to the existence of God through either a mental thought process or through reflection on experience. To take the best-known of all, the argument from design or what came to be known in a later era as the "clockmaker argument," we can deduce from the complexity of the universe the necessity of its having a first principle from which this complexity is derived, and "this we call God."[1]

If Aquinas and many others before and since have believed that a modest amount of information about God—existence and attributes—can be ascertained through the use of reason unaided by revelation, the opposite point of view has since at least the time of Ockham been staunchly maintained. Ockham insists that knowledge of God can only be derived from revelation. It is clear to Ockham that we cannot know God directly in the way in which we know a table, for example, because we cannot have direct experience of God through the use of our unaided intellect. God is not an object of experience in that way. We can only know God because God has revealed the self of God to us. For both Aquinas and Ockham, as we may have discovered by the little eavesdropping we have done, faith is a gift of God that is not dependent on or somehow achieved through the collaboration of human reason. But Aquinas does insist that knowledge of God is truly "knowledge" (*scientia*), while it cannot be for Ockham, since he thinks that knowledge exists only where there is evidence, and the truths of Christianity are not matters for which there is any evidence other than the word of God.[2] For Aquinas, the word of God in Scrip-

---

[1] Aquinas's views on the possibility of this kind of knowledge should not be overstated. See *Contra Gentiles* I/4 for his clearly minimalist optimism about the extent of reason's capacity to know God.

[2] On this, see Marilyn McCord Adams, *William of Ockham*, 2 vols. (Notre Dame, IN: University of Notre Dame Press, 1987). Especially important here is chapter 22, "Faith and Reason," 961–1010.

ture and the authority of the Church produce knowledge, while Ockham insists that we would have to have evident knowledge about God, and this kind of knowledge is not available to us. For Ockham, there are only three ways in which we can attain knowledge of anything. It must be "self-evident or known by experience or proved by the authority of Sacred Scripture."[3]

The first two of Ockham's three ways of knowing sound remarkably similar to the criteria A. J. Ayer laid down in *Language, Truth and Logic*, though the third places him in a different world altogether and enables us at this point to paint a picture of what is at stake in the debates over faith in more recent times. There are, on the one hand, the late nineteenth-century disputes between neo-scholastics and neo-Thomists over the degree to which the act of faith is an intellectual act and, if it is to some degree, whether this does not mean that there can be a kind of "natural faith" distinct from true, supernatural faith. And then there are the approaches of both Catholic and Protestant thinkers that stress the spiritual or sometimes even the affective inspiration of faith.[4] From this perspective, faith begins and perhaps ends in a personal experience of God in Jesus Christ. While Catholic thinkers will be more likely to go on to see this personal experience leading to the acceptance of the authority of the Church in pronouncing dogmatically, Protestant voices are more likely to hear the authority of Scripture

---

[3] Sent. I, dist. 30, q. 1. I am grateful for clarifications suggested to me on this point by my colleague John Slotemaker, though any remaining errors are, of course, my own. What is at stake here is the definition of *scientia*. Ockham believes we can know things, but in the case of knowledge of God, only through revelation. Thomas imagines he is faithful to Aristotle's idea of knowledge, but only by expanding what "knowledge" can mean beyond the Aristotelian categories.

[4] Whose classical exposition is the view of Friedrich Schleiermacher that faith begins in "a feeling of absolute dependence." See *The Christian Faith* (Edinburgh: T & T Clark, 1928), 12–18.

generating the assent of faith, or in later and more liberal forms, to rely on feeling as its basis. Like the differences between such as Aquinas and Ockham, however, agreement is much greater and more fundamental than disagreement. All agree that there is both an intellectual and a spiritual (for want of a better word) component to the experience of faith. The dispute is over how to balance the two.

Though Aquinas and Ockham differ only to a degree, the issues they raise open up questions of deep significance for thinking about faith today. In particular, they constrain us to think about the *source* of faith. If we imagine with Aquinas that there is a component, however limited, of unaided intellectual activity in arriving at some knowledge of God, then there is some basis for the belief that dialogue with the secular world about religious realities is quite possible. Whoever is possessed of intellect is at least in principle open to persuasion that there is a God and that this God possesses certain attributes. Indeed, lying behind the entirety of Aquinas's writings is the conviction that Christian philosophy and theology are perfecting the work of the great pagan philosophers. If we side with Ockham and are persuaded that all knowledge of God and hence any faith is supernatural, deriving from a supernatural gift of grace, then we may value the pagan philosophers but we will see a great divide between what today we would call secular and religious thought.[5] Both thinkers, of course, were in complete agreement that the fullness of Christian faith lies in a free and unmerited gift of God and is not the fruit of human intellect. But in their different ways each competes for the attention of today's Christian. Ockham's belief that faith begins and ends in God's self-revelation to us appeals to our individualism, but

[5] On the relation of both Aquinas and Ockham to the legacy of the pagan philosophers, see Alfred J. Freddoso, "Ockham on Faith and Reason," in *The Cambridge Companion to Ockham*, ed. Paul Vincent Spade (Cambridge: Cambridge University Press, 1999), 326–49.

Aquinas's insistence that there is the possibility of continuity between pagan and Christian philosophy resonates with today's preference for understanding faith in more universalistic categories. Ockham gives us God's free gift and Aquinas gives us a way to think about the salvation of the nonbeliever. On the other hand, removing natural knowledge of God from the equation, as Ockham does, takes away any possibility of thinking of Plato or Aristotle as Christians *avant la lettre*, which some at least might think returns to them their intellectual integrity. It also dramatically saps the energy from apologetics, which classically has its focus on persuading the unbeliever to believe.

When we consider more recent Catholic and Protestant attempts to clarify the act of faith we see that they are all concerned with *Christian* faith and, in the case of neo-scholastic and neo-Thomist writings, of a distinctly Catholic version of that faith, as indeed were the medievals. To anticipate for a moment, thinkers as different in their outlook on St. Thomas as Jean Bainvel[6] and Pierre Rousselot[7] would be in entire agreement that the dogmatic teachings of the Catholic Church are an important component in a fully actualized faith. This would not suit a Protestant perspective, but the insistence on a component of external authority is just as present in its more evangelical forms, this time in the dependence on biblical revelation. What the two have in common is a deep suspicion of purely private faith, that is, of a more mystical or "spiritual" form of religious experience. Because it eschews external authority, mysticism escapes control, whether that of the Scripture principle or that of ecclesiastical magisterium. While none of these thinkers would have expressed themselves openly about the status of non-Christian faith, if any such thing would have

---

[6] Jean Bainvel, *Faith and the Act of Faith* (St. Louis, MO: Herder, 1926).

[7] Pierre Rousselot, *The Eyes of Faith* (New York: Fordham University Press, 1990).

crossed their minds, we shall in time have to raise the question ourselves of what might be the status of such faith once we put aside the humanly constructed boundaries of ecclesiastical authority or Scripture. Much more close to home, there is also the question of what any of them would have made of the overused but still largely accurate slogan of millennial perspectives on faith, "I'm spiritual but I'm not religious."

The Romantic Imagination

As we begin to think about the phenomenon of the human imagination, it might be good to do one more little piece of eavesdropping. Since everyone gets the heaven they imagine, it will be no surprise to encounter Mary Shelley (1797–1851), William Wordsworth (1770–1850), Samuel Taylor Coleridge (1772–1834), and many other Romantics spending their eternity in an Alpine meadow, even if it has the quintessentially English River Wye flowing gently through it and a beautiful ruined abbey that might seem to the trained eye a little too Northern Gothic for Switzerland. Details, details. Let's listen in:

Shelley: *You know, Coleridge, I am not too sure that Wordsworth wouldn't be happier off on his own somewhere. His "sublime" is so English! Pretty, even quaint, and giving rise to solemn thoughts no doubt, but perhaps just a little too provincial. Too many daffodils, not enough opium, I say. My Alpine setting in* Frankenstein, *you will remember, was a place of good and evil. It paid the rent, but I must say that I am delighted not to be worried that a monster might appear to spoil our lunch.*

Coleridge: *My dear Mary, I agree about Wordsworth, and that's the reason that relations between us cooled off considerably as I grew a little older and wiser. He didn't take too kindly to my efforts in* Biographia Literaria *to put his minor genius in its place by explaining that much of what passed for imagination was, in fact, mere fancy. I seem to recall him murmuring, "damn-*

*ing with faint praise" or some such phrase. All I meant to sug-
gest was that his extraordinary talent sometimes drifted away
from the creative genius that consists in bringing into the world
a new vision of the whole and is not to be confused with the pretty
ornamentation of this or that detail.*

Shelley: *I have always wondered if you would have been equally
critical of my work. There is a great deal of mere fancy in my
picture of the monster, but a lot of the more serious stuff I think
I drew in some way from your influence. Ever since as a little
girl I hid behind the parlor sofa to hear you recite your "Rime of
the Ancient Mariner" I have been slowly coming to appreciate
the foolish bravado of those scientists who imagine they have the
power of life over death. So the details of my story may count as
fancy—and whose do not?—but the point of it all, the moral of
the story, is something I meant to be much larger. "What does
it really mean to be human?" I was asking. "And what power
should and does the human have the right to exercise over the
limits of humanity?" Before my time, you have to admit.*

Coleridge: *Well, of course, that's why your little story has survived
so long and has inspired so many others, not all of them laudable
I am afraid, and none of them up to the imaginative standard you
set. Imagination is a possession of all human beings, even if they
do not all take full advantage of it. But the artist is the one who
can create a narrative that is its own thing but at the same time
resonates with that sense of the whole that the human imagination at its best can feel, if it cannot always grasp it. Indeed, the
work of artistic genius is most often the way that those who do
not possess the genius can come close to the imaginative grasp
of the whole that brings enormous spiritual satisfaction. That
is, I would put it even stronger, our encounter with the sublime,
the absolute, what others might even call the divine.*

Shelley: *Poor old Wordsworth talked about it a lot, wrote about it
a lot, but didn't quite get it, I think I hear you saying. It's like
that phrase that "professors of creative writing," whatever that*

is, invented to encourage their students, long after we had gradu-
ated to our Alpine meadow. "Show, don't tell," I think it was.

Coleridge: *Quite. Which is why, by the way—and this is between*
us—I wish people read my poetry more and my critical writings
less. All those letters and notebooks published. Too bad! Like poor
old Emerson, though he didn't have much in the way of poetry
to distract people. And as for Biographia Literaria, *how I wish*
I had never started it. Though I am pleased that my distinction
between fancy and imagination has survived, even if I did crib
it from some minor German philosopher. I hope he doesn't show
up here in our Alpine meadow.

When we ask about the imagination, under the influence of
Romantic poets and writers like Mary Shelley and Samuel
Taylor Coleridge, the very first thing we need to do is to disabuse ourselves of the common or garden conversational use
of the word. "Oh, come on, there's no such thing; it's just your
imagination," or—at an elite level—Bertrand Russell's injunc-
tion to "imagine a golden mountain, now imagine a golden
mountain existing—is there any difference?" We can encounter,
then, in the most conversational of everyday language and in
some of the most arcane twentieth-century philosophizing—
a British analytical philosopher attempting a disproof of
Anselm's ontological argument for the existence of God—
plainly erroneous use of the word "imagination." In
Coleridgean terminology that we will shortly explore a little
further, what my unlettered friend and Bertrand Russell have
in common is mistaking for imagination what is, in fact, mere
fancy. In working-class northern England a couple of generations ago, and perhaps still now, they got it right. If you were
to throw out to someone a far-fetched idea or an entrancing
but unlikely possibility, like dangling before them all the good
things that might follow from winning the lottery, a dreamy
look might come over the face, accompanied by the words,

"Eeeh, fancy that!" In other words, how wonderful it would be if that were the case, but it's clearly not.

It may seem a bit of a leap from Aquinas and Ockham to Samuel Taylor Coleridge and the company of Romantic poets, but if we are going to trace the development of the idea of religious faith into the twentieth century, it is not such a detour as we might imagine. While the Romantics taken as a whole were not exactly textbook Christians, they certainly had a sense of the sublime, the absolute, even at times the divine. They were, in fact, the first post-Enlightenment women and men of letters who confronted transcendence without embarrassment and wrote of religion without contempt. They may have found inspiration in the heavens rather than in Heaven, and certainly not in the Bible, but they were possessed of what more traditionally religious people might consider to be the single most important of human qualities, a sense of transcendence, of something far greater and more mysterious than our puny human selves. The enemy of the Romantic spirit is not religion, not even Christianity, but the far different spirit of Enlightenment rationalism. In this regard, they could unite with Christians in defense against a common enemy, and they provide an excellent starting point for examining the common purposes of literature and religion.

Coleridge's *Biographia Literaria*[8] has to be one of the most frustrating books one could encounter. It divides neatly into two halves, which do not hold together well. The first half is a pure tease, a promise to unfold a theory of the imagination that never materializes. The second part, mostly about Wordsworth, becomes so interesting to the writer that he forgets what he set out to do in the first half. Halfway into the book, on the verge of getting to the point, Coleridge invents a letter from a friend to whom Coleridge claims he has sent the manuscript of his great theory of the imagination. In effect, he has the

---

[8] Samuel Taylor Coleridge, *Biographia Literaria* (London: n.p., 1817), 95–96.

friend advise him that the theory is too complicated for most human beings to follow, and he should drop it, at least for now. Barely disguising his relief, Coleridge says that he will instead offer a short version of the argument. This turns out to be two paragraphs, very famous paragraphs in the history of Romantic literary criticism but also a tease, though of a different kind. Having cajoled his reader through a lengthy hundred pages or so with the promise of a theory that doesn't appear, he substitutes a brief and positively gnomic utterance that has had a huge and probably disproportionate effect on subsequent thinkers.[9] Coleridge begins by distinguishing the primary and secondary imaginations from "mere fancy." The primary, he says, "I hold to be the living power and prime agent of all human perception, and as a repetition in the finite mind of the eternal act of creation in the infinite I AM." The secondary imagination is "an echo of the former," which "dissolves, diffuses, dissipates, in order to re-create. . . . It struggles to idealize and to unify." "Fancy, on the contrary," he continues, "has no other counters to play with but fixities and definites" and "is indeed no other than a mode of memory emancipated from the order of time and space." This is about all we get, together with the never-fulfilled promise of a "critical essay on the uses of the supernatural in poetry."

Coleridge's brief remarks on the imagination have occasioned an enormous outpouring of efforts to explain his ideas and account for their influence. The best source for cutting through the forest of arguments and counterarguments, however, may actually be the words of Edgar Allen Poe, who wrote in an unsigned review that "Imagination is, possibly, in man, a lesser degree of the creative power in God." "The sentiment

---

[9] For a thorough debunking of the originality of Coleridge's theory of the imagination that nevertheless recognizes the influence his words had in channeling German philosophy to an Anglo world that did not read German, see Mary Warnock, *Imagination* (Berkeley: University of California Press, 1976), 72–102.

of Poesy," he writes, "is the sense of the beautiful, and of the sublime, and of the mystical." It is that which gives rise to aesthetic appreciation of natural beauty and of the power and majesty of the heavens and, inextricably intermingled with this, "the unconquerable desire—to know." Poetry, then, is "the practical result in certain individuals" of the sentiment of Poesy. This practical result is the secondary imagination of which Coleridge speaks. The capacity of imaginative genius in some creative individuals that enables them to fashion a work of art is dependent on but also builds on the capacity of the imagination that is the possession of all human beings. But the gestation period that the secondary imagination requires to work on the primary may be quite extended and is never instantaneous. We shall shortly encounter something very similar in the work of Henry James, when he discloses in his preface to *The American* in the New York Edition of his novels that he had come up with an idea for a novel and "must have dropped it for a time into the deep well of unconscious cerebration."[10] James, being no Romantic, substitutes a suspicious-sounding neuroscientific reference to brain activity, not to the divine or the sublime. Quite unlike his psychologist brother William, who was content with something much more Romantic.[11]

While Romanticism is sometimes dismissed as airy-fairy mental meandering among nature images and soft-sounding quasi-mysticism, it is more accurately understood as a corrective to the materialism of much of Enlightenment thought,

[10] Henry James, *Literary Criticism: French Writers, Other European Writers, The Prefaces to the New York Edition* (New York: Literary Classics of the United States, n.d.), 1055. I am indebted for this reference to James Volant Baker, *The Sacred River: Coleridge's Theory of the Imagination* (Baton Rouge: Louisiana State University Press, 1957), 122.

[11] For a trenchant discussion of the misreading of neuroscience, see Marilynne Robinson, *The Givenness of Things: Essays* (New York: Farrar, Strauss and Giroux, 2015), especially the essay on "Humanism," 1–16.

without returning to traditional religious concepts.[12] Looking past the harshness of Coleridge's judgment on Wordsworth, the great poet was trying to capture a sense of that which lies beyond the individual or even beneath the natural world. It is easy for us to label it "the transcendent," and so long as we do not smuggle back in the Jewish or Christian God, not at all inaccurate. The domestic beauty of the River Wye on which Wordsworth meditated impressed him with a sense of human insignificance over against the whole. In the mechanism and materialism of Enlightenment thought there is a movement toward the neuroscientific temptation to imagine that when we can identify brain wave patterns in human thought processes, we have explained human thought. The Romantic resistance to this reductionism does not depend on a traditional belief in a deity and has little if any of the ethical dimension of Christian faith, but it is one with theological thinking in its commitment to a sense of a whole that exists independently of human thought processes but which is encountered through the human imagination. As William Blake put it in a clear challenge to all forms of positivism, "The tree which moves some to tears of joy is in the eyes of others only a green thing that stands in the way. Some see nature all ridicule and deformity . . . and some scarce see nature at all. But to the eyes of the man of imagination, nature is imagination itself." Moreover, he wrote, "I know of no other Christianity and of no other Gospel than the liberty both of body & mind to exercise the Divine Arts of Imagination."

For romantic thinkers like Blake, Shelley, Coleridge, and Wordsworth, the human imagination is the supreme faculty we possess, though the artist has a particular responsibility to it. It certainly does not replace or displace reason; on the con-

---

[12] Eugene McCarraher traces in excellent fashion what he calls the "sacramental dialect" of Romanticism in "We Have Never Been Disenchanted," *The Hedgehog Review* 17, no. 3 (Fall 2015): 86–100.

trary, it enables reason to see clearly.[13] The Romantics in general, but none more clearly than Blake, were able to distinguish between an instrumental reason that reduced everything to mere information and a more dynamic form of reason that conspired with the imagination to see through appearances to some grasp of what lay beyond. This imaginative capacity is a universal human possession, they believed. But as we have seen in the work of Coleridge, the artist is the one who possesses the gift of quickening the human imagination. The creative imagination of the artist produces a work of art that enables and enriches the everyday imagination. Through their work we are all led to some apprehensions of the infinite or the sublime that lies beyond the mere appearances of this present world. When we describe it this way, we can see why the term "sacramental" is particularly accurate to describe the Romantics' view of reality. It would, however, be a mistake to dichotomize this world and the real world, as big a mistake as a Christian would make who thought of God as a reality only to be encountered beyond this world. The imagination finds the holy, if we may be allowed to use this word, both the holy of Christian faith and the holy of the Romantic imagination, present in this world and met through the powers of the human imagination.

In the course of the nineteenth century, the Catholic Church saw a return to a form of what came to be known as neo-scholasticism in Catholic orthodoxy. This represented a return to understanding faith as a cognitive act as much if not more than one of the will or the imagination, supported by a deeply unhistorical appropriation of the work of St. Thomas. When the reaction to this approach began to set in at the end of the nineteenth century, both in the highly suspect activities of what Pope Pius X would call "Modernism . . . the mother of all heresies," and in a new reading of Thomas as a product of his

---

[13] Ibid., 95.

historical context, it became time for a new approach to under-standing faith as a product of a healthy relationship between intellect and imagination, a nascent theory of the act of faith whose development we shall track in the next chapter.

■ ■ ■ ■ ■ ■   *Chapter Two*   ■ ■ ■ ■ ■ ■

Faith in the Modern World

The Eyes of Faith: Pierre Rousselot's **Via Media**

Among the countless human tragedies of World War I, the greatest loss to the world of Catholic theology was certainly the death of Pierre Rousselot. Born in 1878, he became a Jesuit in 1895, wrote two dissertations, on the intellectualism of St. Thomas and on love in the Middle Ages, that were both eventually published, was given the chair of dogmatic theology at the Institut Catholique in Paris at the age of thirty-one, was called up for military service at the outset of the Great War, and was killed in battle in April 1915. His writings on faith are contained in two short essays on "the eyes of faith" and another in response to critics of his position, written a couple of years later.[1] His efforts to find a middle path between two quite different approaches to the faith and reason question led to his being attacked from both sides, often enough an indication that you must be doing something right.

While it would be a mistake to juxtapose the views of Aquinas and Ockham, to turn back to them for just a moment, there are

---

[1] Pierre Rousselot, "Les yeux de la foi," *Recherches de Science Religieuse* 1 (1910): 241–59 and 444–75, and "Réponse à deux attaques," *Recherches de Science Religieuse* 5 (1914): 57–69. The English translation is *The Eyes of Faith*, with the first two essays translated by Joseph Donceel, with an introduction by John M. McDermott, and the "Answer to Two Attacks" translated by Avery Dulles (New York: Fordham University Press, 1990).

19

significant contrasts between their theories of the faith/knowl-
edge relationship. One can see in their differing perspectives
how each stresses something that, when caricatured, becomes
an unbalanced view of faith that would not satisfy either of
them. But over time, two very different understandings of the
dynamics of faith did in fact emerge in Catholic theology that
to a degree displayed such caricatures. On the one hand, there
were those thinkers who believed that faith came before any
recognition of its rationality. Maurice Blondel and the Catholic
modernist thinkers like Alfred Loisy and George Tyrrell can
serve as examples of this perspective. Others, on the contrary,
were convinced that some intellectual recognition of the credibility of faith had to precede the act of faith itself. Here we
would find exemplary the work of Ambrose Gardeil[2] and Jean
Bainvel.[3] The latter group would maintain that we cannot
believe unless we have formulated at least some preliminary
intellectual understanding of what is involved in believing
(credibility) and, perhaps, have seen that we *ought* to believe
(in scholastic terminology, "credentity"). The former group is
just as sure that unless we possess faith, we do not have the
means to assent intellectually to the truths of faith. Faith is the
necessary condition of credibility.

It does not take a particularly sophisticated thinker to see that
the intellect/faith relationship is actually a fine example of the
chicken and the egg problem, and it was this insight—though
not this image—that lay behind Rousselot's brilliant voyage
between the Scylla of neo-scholasticism and the Charybdis of
voluntarism. Evidently, we cannot make an act of faith in something that does not have at least some intellectual component,
or we would be putting our faith in nothing, but we cannot

[2] Ambrose Gardeil, *La crédibilité et l'apologétique* (Paris: Gabalda, 1908).

[3] Jean Vincent Bainvel, *Faith and the Act of Faith* (St. Louis, MO: Herder,
1926). Originally published in French in 1898, and in a revised second edition
in 1908.

understand faith as something to which we are led, even in a preliminary way, by the intellectual credibility of the content of the faith. What Rousselot saw so clearly was that attempting to establish the chronological priority of one or the other was doomed to failure. Convinced that his position was entirely faithful to Aquinas, Rousselot argued holistically that all components of the act of faith are always already at work together. As he writes, "*Perception of credibility and belief in truth are identically the same act.*"[4]

Rousselot's balancing act left no room for what the scholastics had called "natural knowledge," still less for natural faith, but didn't entirely close the door on unbelievers. If "perception of credibility and belief in truth are identically the same act," then there can be no preliminary state of natural faith, no awareness of credibility awaiting the onset of credentity that would then elicit faith. Faith and the intellectual assent that is simultaneous with the act of faith are a vision, a sudden seeing, that is possible only because of the light that God shines on us. In this light, the eyes of faith are opened. On the one hand, this seems to leave the greater part of the human race out in the cold. On the other, locating the light of faith in the synthesizing capacity of the intellect reveals a more generous prospect, one in which, as later thinkers will say, grace is not something added on to nature but a dimension of the graced nature that is the human person. Thinking along these lines, one can imagine the claim that faith is the final perfection of human nature (a thoroughly Thomistic sentiment) and that growing in humanity is growing toward God (a distinctly Irenaean view). Hence the traditional view that all humane relationships outside the context of faith are a preparation for the Gospel and, perhaps, the Rahnerian insight that, because God's will to the salvation of all cannot be frustrated by circumstance but only by the free choice of the individual, all

---

[4] Rousselot, *The Eyes of Faith*, 31 (author's emphasis).

human beings are somehow confronted with the choice to embrace the mystery of the whole.

Rousselot's analysis of the act of faith leans heavily on Aquinas's concept of the *lumen fidei*, which we can rightly see as the free gift of God without being led to an extrinsicist view. The light of faith is the free gift of God's grace, but of course it is not magical. The gift of grace has to be understood in terms of human psychology. To take one of Rousselot's analogies, it is a bit like turning to Shakespeare's *Hamlet*, which we have read or seen many times with great enjoyment but without truly grasping the meaning of the whole, and this time around we have something like what the ethicist Paul Ramsey calls "the aha moment." As Ramsey saw it, we "get" it when "the penny drops" or "the light goes on." Where does this sudden insight come from? Rousselot would say, with Aquinas, that it arises from the synthetic activity of the intellect, that which allows us to see the whole as whole, and that this is the light of faith given to us by a free act of divine grace. Rousselot concludes that "nothing stands in the way of our affirming, with St. Thomas, that it is the light of faith that shows that we must believe," and he asks if this involves us in some kind of vicious circle (chicken and egg!).

> Only if we claim to demonstrate a proposition as certain by means of another that is as yet undemonstrated and that depends in turn on the former. But there is no trace of a vicious circle if we say that affirming some proposition requires that we possess the spiritual faculty that makes the connection of its terms clear, the synthetic activity that unites those terms, or, to speak as older authors did, the light that illuminates them.[5]

The synthesizing faculty of the intellect does not provide us with knowledge of Hamlet that we previously did not possess,

---

[5] Ibid.

but it enables us to grasp the meaning of Hamlet. The light of faith does not clarify for us any natural knowledge we might possess about the city of Rome, to borrow another of Rousselot's analogies, but—at least for the Catholic whom he is imagining—in its light we see Rome as the Church, "the mother of the children of God, the spouse of Christ, the teacher of salvation."[6]

The Personalist Turn

In the century that has come and gone since Rousselot wrote, reflection on the act of faith in major sectors of Catholic and Protestant thought has come to emphasize the impact of a personal relationship with Jesus Christ as its instigation and motivation. While this was not the way in which Rousselot described the dynamics of faith, this more contemporary approach seems to be largely consistent with his vision. Rousselot continued to insist on an intellectual component to the act of faith, but in what he saw to be a view entirely faithful to the thought of Aquinas he gave equal stress to the role of the will, moved by God's grace to assent to faith. In what circumstances do we encounter the grace of God that leads to the light of faith shining on and enlightening our grasp of the meaning of the whole? Not, certainly, through intellectual persuasion. But also, in most cases, not commonly in some mystical encounter with God, the *mysterium tremendum et fascinans*.[7] In all probability, and here we may hear echoes of Ockham, in the person of Jesus Christ as the revelation of God, but, echoing Aquinas, requiring an intellectual component, if there is to be anything at all to which we can give the assent of faith. In the end, Rousselot is rightly considered an important corrective to the intellectual positivism of neo-scholasticism, for which the intellect somehow takes the lead in a decision to commit to faith.

---

[6] Rousselot, *The Eyes of Faith*, 33.

[7] Rudolf Otto, *The Idea of the Holy* (Oxford: Oxford University Press, 1958).

The turn to faith as personal encounter is evident among twentieth-century Catholics in the thought of Karl Adam, Romano Guardini, Marie-Dominique Chenu, Karl Rahner, and many others. Among Protestant theologians a similar orientation appears in the writings of Dietrich Bonhoeffer, H. Richard Niebuhr, and Jürgen Moltmann. To explore just a little further some of the important implications of this personalist turn we will focus here, on the Catholic side, on Jean Mouroux's book *I Believe: The Personal Structure of Faith*[8] and, on the Protestant side, Niebuhr's posthumously published text, *Faith on Earth.*[9]

Mouroux's short but important book was written under the influence of the French theological movement that came to be known as *la nouvelle théologie*—itself inspired by Rousselot— but steps beyond it in its consistent focus on the personal dimension of faith, both the personhood of the believer and the personhood of the object of belief. Like Rousselot before him, Mouroux saw his work as an explication of Aquinas that corrected the rigidities of the reigning neo-scholastic intellectualist orthodoxy, but he moved further than Rousselot from attention to the role of the intellect. For Mouroux, everything begins and ends with the person in whom one believes. Faith, he writes, is "a simple act": "Analysis will show therein the presence of will, of thought and spiritual feelings, but all this is within the unity of one vital act, the act of a person who united himself with another person."[10] Any real contact with any person at all is effected in "a spiritual contact and by a phenomenon of communion," and, "in the case of living faith, the whole spiritual being throws itself open to welcome the God who calls it." And so, echoing Rousselot, "we can see above all that love

[8] Jean Mouroux, *I Believe: The Personal Structure of Faith*, trans. Michael Turner (New York: Sheed and Ward, 1959). Originally published in 1948 by Les Editions du Cerf as *Je Crois en Toi: structure personelle de la foi*.

[9] H. Richard Niebuhr, *Faith on Earth: An Inquiry into the Structure of Human Faith*, ed. Richard R. Niebuhr (New Haven, CT: Yale University Press, 1989).

[10] Mouroux, *I Believe*, 42.

and knowledge are *inseparable* in this act, because both are essential activities of the human person." It is "the human being as a unity which is given, for it is neither the will nor the intellect which exists but the man."[11]

The personalist account of faith draws an analogy between how we come to know, love, and trust another person, and how we come to know, love, and trust God. If we think about how we have come to know and love the people closest to us in our lives—lovers, family, and friends—we know that the bonds between us are not a product of information we received ahead of meeting them or, indeed, in most cases of an immediate affective unity when we first meet them. Rather, these bonds were and are an ongoing encounter between two people in all their complexity and idiosyncrasies in which ideas and emotions and feelings play a part but on which the love between the two is in no way dependent. The heart of a loving relationship is not agreement on this or that, or sentimental or even erotic attraction, but self-revelation. The openness of one to the other is what is common to the richest expressions of love of whatever variety. As Andrew Greeley put it somewhat ungrammatically, "We win the other by surrendering ourself to him. We get the other by giving ourself to him and he, in his turn, conquers us by surrendering to us."[12] In the case of coming to know, love, and trust God, "The act of faith is the *gift of himself* which the created person makes to the Uncreated Being, thus it is knowledge which is brought about by love."[13]

Mouroux pursues the analogy in his examination of the obscurity of faith. Beginning once again from a phenomenology of human loving, he suggests that the act of faith is

---

[11] Ibid., 43.

[12] Andrew Greeley, *The Friendship Game* (New York: Doubleday, 1970). I am indebted to Anne Krane for bringing this early work by Greeley to my attention.

[13] Mouroux, *I Believe*, 46–47.

obscure "because it is the self-revelation by one person to another," and this is not something that can simply be grasped by discursive reason. Moreover, coming to appreciate the existence and value of another person is not something that discursive reason can engineer. This is an affair of the heart, but even here there is obscurity. Again, as we know from our own experience, however much we love another person or come to know him or her in great depth, there is always something at the center that is inaccessible, even to love. Perceiving the value of another, writes Mouroux, "is not the luminous penetration of an inner reality." Rather, it is "a sort of *contact* and *coincidence* with the being discovered," which is open to "indefinite investigation" but is "in part opaque and resistant to reason."[14]

If all efforts to love another involve a measure of obscurity, how much more so when the object of love is God: "Faith is obscure because it is the revelation of a *divine* person through a *human* testimony."[15] Because the testimony is human it is inadequate to that to which it testifies; it is "our only source of light" but "it hides God at the same time as it reveals him."[16] Moreover, the obscurity is compounded by human sinfulness. As fallen human beings, both our intellect and our will are wounded and we are in search of an absent God, not the God visible in the Garden of Eden. And yet we have certitude alongside obscurity: "Faith is certain, not because it comprises the *evidence of a thing seen*, but because it is the *assent to a Person who sees*."[17] Mouroux quotes Aquinas in personalist mode, drawing parallels between human interpersonality and the act of faith in God:

[14] Ibid., 51.
[15] Ibid.
[16] Ibid., 52.
[17] Ibid., 54.

> Everyone who believes assents to someone's words; and thus,
> in any form of belief, it seems that it is *the person to whose words*
> *the assent is given*, who is of principal importance and, as it
> were, the end; while the individual truths through which one
> assents to that person are secondary.[18]

There could hardly be a clearer assertion of the priority of the
heart over the mind in the act of faith.

That the act of faith is motivated by love and is not primarily
an intellectual assent to a truth or set of truths is what divides
what we may like to call a modern from a pre-modern understanding, though we should be wary of consigning everything
before Rousselot to the scrap heap. As the quotation from
Aquinas above reveals, the contemporary grasp of what is
involved in the act of faith has ancient roots, though what we
are calling here the pre-modern theory, especially in its hardest
versions in nineteenth-century neo-scholasticism, also claims
Aquinas for its authority. But the differences are stark, if under-
standable. The pre-modern or intellectualist position insists
that the possibility of loving God requires some knowledge,
however minimal, of what God is (credibility) and that therefore one *ought* to love God (credentity), before the will can
move to the act of faith. The modern view argues that loving
anyone, including and especially God, *must* begin with a personal encounter that will then unfold dynamically in a way in
which the intellect will be involved.

The implications of the more phenomenological approach
to describing the act of faith that imply an analogical or iso-
morphic relationship between human loving and loving God
become clearer in the writings of H. Richard Niebuhr, most
particularly in his posthumously published text, *Faith on Earth*.
Niebuhr begins from a process of reflection on self and human
knowing, identifying our age as an age of faith in science. As

---

[18] ST IIa-IIae, xi, I.

he points out, relatively few people actually understand the scientific world, but they take a lot on trust, believing the scientist and so believing the world is as the scientist says it is. While this examination of the role of trust in human knowing is a long way from the knowledge of God acquired in faith, Niebuhr suggests that it may lead us toward appreciating "how social is our faith in God, how it includes acknowledgment of Him as a faithful person, and also includes truth-relationship between selves and companions."[19]

Niebuhr starts from the assertion that all human knowing is based on faith and trust in another, in a community, about something or other. He follows Buber's famous notion of the I-Thou relationship but insists that in the I-Thou encounter there is also always an It, that is, "some object with which and about which we can communicate."[20] This kind of faith or trust is necessary but, because it is the possession of sinful human beings, always broken. Even faith in God is broken in this way, tinged with doubt or fear or anxiety. In our I-Thou relationships we are aware, says Niebuhr, of the transcendent or unconditioned ground of the possibility of these relationships, of the radical source of our being and of all beings, but this awareness is grasped in fear or awe, until it is perceived as "some trust in that God in whom Jesus Christ trusted as Father."[21] Prior to faith we recognize the Transcendent but we do not trust it. This is "natural religion," and in this moment our task is Promethean, says Niebuhr, quoting Bertrand Russell. Russell's conviction of the nonexistence of divine purposes spares us "the necessity for that attitude of impotent hatred which every brave and humane man would otherwise be called upon to adopt towards the Almighty Tyrant."[22] So, if

[19] Niebuhr, *Faith on Earth*, 42.

[20] Ibid., 47.

[21] Ibid., 64–65.

[22] Bertrand Russell, *The Scientific Outlook* (New York: W. W. Norton, 1927), 301, quote in Niebuhr, *Faith on Earth*, 72.

we believe in this God of natural religion, we fear this God. The contrast is between Prometheus and Job, whose "honest questioning" is "without fear oppressed by guilt."

> The brave man of the Promethean type confronts a distrusted transcendent reality with courage; the brave man trusting stands before God like Job asking for an answer; the fearsome man confronts the distrusted Transcendent with trembling; the fearsome man full of trust is awed but not cowed and there is joy in his awe.[23]

While natural religion is marked by a faith of fear, suspicion, and lack of trust, it cannot exist without faith, even broken faith, but it can be transformed, says Niebuhr, by faith in the present-day Christ. Faith exists within churches, but it is not synonymous with or dependent on churches. "It is not an affair of organizations, of doctrines, of beliefs, of rites" and, in a critique that recalls Rousselot, "neither is it individual piety." On the contrary, it is "the interpersonal movement of faith that centers in the person of Jesus Christ." We must start from the experience now of the risen Christ, then work backward to trust in him as a historical figure, to those who trusted in him. It is our living relationship with the risen Christ now that enables us to reconstruct the whole life of faith. We cannot come to faith by starting with the historical reconstructions of the life of Jesus of Nazareth or the doctrines of churches, says Niebuhr, in remarkable agreement with the entire medieval tradition, not to mention the modern corrections to the neo-scholastic vision presented in the work of Rousselot and Mouroux.

The Catholic tradition represented by Mouroux in particular could not go the whole way with Niebuhr. They certainly concur in seeing the ground of faith in a personal encounter with Christ, and probably also with Niebuhr's account of the

---

[23] Niebuhr, *Faith on Earth*, 72.

reconstruction of faith beginning with the risen Christ in the present day and then working retroactively to a richer appropriation of the history of trust in Christ that constitutes Tradition, as Catholics see it. But the harsh juxtaposition of Prometheus and Job offends against Catholicism's more generous appreciation of the extent of divine grace. Mouroux quotes Louis Richard to good effect: "To every soul . . ., even one reared in atheism, grace offers as an object, as something to be loved above all things, under whatever name the soul describes such an end to itself . . . offers that Reality of absolute goodness, which merits all our love and is able to save our life."[24] From the Catholic perspective, the sinful human being who is without explicit faith in God is nevertheless oriented to the transcendent in some way, however inchoate. Even believers may have profound depth of faith while "the concepts and formulas which express this commitment in an explicit affirmation can often be extraordinarily poor and inaccurate."[25] How much more difficult for the unbeliever who is possessed of "images and concepts made for something quite different." God, however, says Mouroux, does not ask of the believer more than can be given, and so "the saving movement of the soul, initiated by grace, can pass through formulas, themselves pitifully inadequate, or even glaringly false."[26]

Faith in "a World Come of Age"

Whether the fault is ours or that of the tradition, there is something foreign to the contemporary consciousness in the accounts of the act of faith we have been examining. All the opinions we have so far considered are the products of men

---

[24] Louis Richard, *Le Dogme de la Rédemption* (Paris: Bloud et Gay, 1931), 56–57, quoted by Mouroux, *I Believe*, 75.

[25] Mouroux, *I Believe*, 71.

[26] Ibid., 73–74.

of faith, which is certainly not surprising, since those who possess faith might be likeliest to be able to describe its character. But the consequence is that there is a prevailing assumption that faith, shall we say, is the default condition of human life. While the personalist account of faith, especially that of Mouroux, opens the door to the possibility that there may be faith that does not at all look like faith, and that might seem to be an explicit rejection of *religious* faith, there is nevertheless a sort of presumed transcendental structure of human being that is open to the transcendent.[27] And if God is seen as pure love, as Rahner might put it, the vacuum that would otherwise exist at the heart of the human being is always already filled by God, waiting only to be named.

In the twentieth and perhaps even more so in the twenty-first centuries, the possibility or even inevitability of faith comes to seem very different from the world of the more distant past. There are many reasons why this is so. First, the social context of faith is quite dramatically different from what it once was. Even superficially, the ages of faith made faith easier. Born into faithful practice in a faith community, one could certainly drift into imperfect faith, but the decision not to believe was no small thing, requiring a radical shift of consciousness and often the rejection of the social world one owned. Today, for most people in the West the situation is almost exactly reversed. Whether growing up in a family with some religious identity or not, faith has become an individual decision. Indeed, the millennials who are thought to espouse the creed of "I'm spiritual but not religious" are at the very least rejecting the value of the social framework that aids the faith commitment in times of trial. In Europe to a high degree and increasingly in North America, religious faith is seen as quaint,

---

[27] Mouroux quotes favorably the work of Fr. Claeys-Bouaert, who "has shown how one could really affirm God, while denying him on the level of a certain conceptual formulation" (ibid., 74).

if not bizarre or fanatical, and certainly regressive. In the United States the Nones are not yet the majority, but they are well on the way.[28]

There are a number of other reasons why the calculus of faith is differently configured in our age. The growth in sophistication of scientific inquiry, particularly into neuroscience, seems to make faith unnecessary. The wonder in the face of God's creation is displaced by wonder at the enormous complexity of the universe or the human brain. Second, the awareness that we now possess of the extent of human suffering, past and present, made much more evident by the communications explosion that has shrunk the world, seems sometimes to render faith in God quite obscene. And if not obscene, it threatens to return us to a more primitive world of natural religion in which the God who may or may not exist is a figure who elicits fear and hatred, not love. And third, that same shrinking of the human world that has forced us to confront the extent of human cruelty and suffering has also opened us up to an awareness of the multiplicity of religious belongings, inevitably relativizing any sense of the superiority of our own. We may not be forced to abandon religious faith, but we may be pressed to ask just who this God is in whom we profess to believe. We have encountered the God who is revealed in Christ, professes the Christian, but how much of that God is actually hidden? By what right is Christocentric monotheism made a hermeneutic of human religious longing?

In the face of these kinds of questions it is fitting to bring this account of the act of faith to a close with a brief glance at the ideas of Dietrich Bonhoeffer. In scattered fragments in his *Letters and Papers from Prison*, this young German Lutheran pastor, sitting in a Nazi jail, broached these questions, if not

---

[28] For more information on the phenomenon of the Nones, see the study of the Pew Research Center: http://www.pewresearch.org/fact-tank/2015/05/13/a-closer-look-at-americas-rapidly-growing-religious-nones/.

for the first time, certainly most memorably. When Bonhoeffer writes of "a world come of age" he is pointing to the non-necessity of God in modern life. People do not need to have recourse to God in order to explain or manipulate their daily existence, and to turn to God only to help with the "limit-questions" of life and death seems to Bonhoeffer to be a matter of assigning God a place, of a "God of the gaps" once more. But here is the question: is the non-necessity of God in fact the beginning of the end of faith, or is it—as Bonhoeffer argued—God's gift of freedom and of the world to humanity, to act with full responsibility for the fate of the earth?

Any interpretation of Bonhoeffer's fragments written from prison in occasional letters to his close friend Eberhard Bethge must be highly tentative, as tentative indeed as he indicated to Bethge that his own thoughts were. Nevertheless, his writing is sufficiently suggestive that it invites a response, even perhaps an excited response. Bonhoeffer, like no one before him, faced squarely the non-necessity of God in the modern world and saw it as part of God's plan. Human responsibility for the fate of the earth is exactly that, given into human hands by God, in such a way that God cannot be invoked to fix one thing or explain another. It is our human freedom and responsibility that are at stake. We must act *etsi deus non daretur*, as if God did not exist. Consequently, the whole framework of organized religion becomes questionable, since it shores up an understanding of what God wants of us and what we can ask of God that is frankly alienating. The human person, for Bonhoeffer, is no longer *homo religiosus* but a secular person, though a secular person of faith. Traditional Christian apologetics attacks the world come of age in a way that is unchristian, he writes, "because it confuses Christ with one particular stage in man's religiousness, i.e., with a human law."[29]

---

[29] Dietrich Bonhoeffer, *Letters and Papers from Prison: The Enlarged Edition*, ed. Eberhard Bethge (London: The Folio Society, 2000), 291.

For Bonhoeffer, the object of faith is the suffering Christ as seen in the suffering of the world: "It is not the religious act that makes the Christian, but participation in the sufferings of God in the secular life."[30] In a very interesting passage he refers to various New Testament figures—the shepherds, the wise men, Zacchaeus, Joseph of Arimathea, the centurion of Capernaum, and so on—and comments that "the only thing that is common to all these is their sharing the suffering of God in Christ." "That," he adds, "is their faith," and "Jesus calls men, not to a new religion, but to life."[31] Bonhoeffer's theology is profoundly Christocentric, but the Christ who is at its center is seen in the suffering of the world around us, and true faith in the suffering Christ is evidenced by a commitment to the struggle to overcome human suffering in the here and now.

Reading Bonhoeffer inevitably leads to the question, if faith in Christ is seen in a commitment to overcoming human suffering, and Jesus calls us to new life, not to a new religion, then can we say that those who struggle to overcome human suffering without benefit of explicit Christian faith do indeed possess the one faith that is necessary for salvation? Christian spirituality has always been inclined to see the face of Christ in suffering humanity but less likely to recognize the unbeliever as a person of faith. Bonhoeffer, however, would have us give up the screen of doctrine that the churches imagine is the only way we encounter God in Christ, exchanging it for a purely human commitment to overcoming suffering. No doubt some of his rejection of "religion" had to do with the deplorable performance of the German churches in the face of Nazism, but it is more than this. Faith is to be a disciple of Christ, and Christ came to bring healing and wholeness to suffering humanity. Those who work for this cause are disciples of Christ,

---

[30] Ibid., 323.
[31] Ibid.

even if perhaps they do not know it or would deny it if asked.[32] By uncoupling faith in Christ from "religion" and proposing an understanding of discipleship that does not require any thematized relationship to Christianity, or any other religious tradition for that matter, Bonhoeffer sketches in outline what has become the utterly changed landscape of faith today.

The Problematics of Faith Today

Before Bonhoeffer, no Christian theologian seemed to feel the need to examine the context in which the act of faith takes place. For the medievals, no doubt, the question did not occur because the world they envisaged was a Christian world in which, for the most part, people were born into communities of faith that both nurtured the faith from an early age and sanctioned those who wandered from its path. You were a public unbeliever at your peril, to your immortal soul certainly, but also to a livable life in a social world that would shun you, if not worse. The scholastics and neo-scholastics whose thought we have touched on in the early pages of this chapter did not have to contend with plausible alternate accounts of the world. There was no "secular world" competing with a "religious world." To be an unbeliever was to be an outcast.

In the world we live in today, at least in the global north, the role of context is entirely different. The secularity of the world is simply a given, not in the sense that faith is excluded, but rather in that the vast majority of its citizens manage their lives *etsi deus non daretur*, even the majority of those who would consider themselves to be people of faith. We do not live in an age of faith, though we live in a world in which it is still true

---

[32] Augustine said something similar. See *The City of God*, trans. Henry Bettenson (London and New York: Penguin Classics, 2004), chap. 35, "Of the Sons of the Church Who Are Hidden among the Wicked, and of False Christians within the Church."

that large numbers of people possess faith, though what exactly this faith consists in is not always easy to discern. It is also true that the secular world in which we live is the descendent of Christian and Jewish cultures, while large parts of the world continue to be shaped by religious traditions—especially the varieties of Islam—that reject the idea that the secular world is normative. Even here, however, much of life is shaped by the assumptions of secularity. Believers in God we may be, but for the most part the lives of believers and unbelievers are indistinguishable from one another.

The fundamentally religious shape of the pre-modern world meant that individuals were required to take an attitude to it, whether of faith (for the vast majority) or of rejection of faith (for a tiny minority). Today, in face of the secular world, the challenge is not to take an attitude but to interpret. This distinction is important in the aesthetic response theory of literature proposed by Wolfgang Iser, and we shall return to his thinking in some detail in the next chapter. To anticipate, Iser uses this distinction to signify how fiction might differ from purely informational writing, or indeed—in his somewhat elitist approach—how "real" fiction might be separated from merely "light reading." The latter, or informational texts, he writes, have their meaning or significance formulated in the text and the reader will "adopt an attitude toward the one offered him." In real fiction, however, its greater complexity means that the text offers multiple possible meanings that "are not explicitly formulated," so that "the formulation will take place through the guided activity stimulated in the reader."[33]

It is possible that Iser's distinction between attitude and interpretation may shed some light on our consideration of pre-modern and modern understandings of faith. There is a huge difference between traditional and more contemporary

---

[33] Wolfgang Iser, *The Act of Reading: A Theory of Aesthetic Response* (Baltimore, MD: Johns Hopkins University Press, 1978), 46.

attitudes to the possibility of faith. In ages past as one can see even from the cursory glance we have taken at the development of thinking about faith, the action of the spirit was assumed to elicit a simple response. The individual was moved to the act of faith by some combination of intellectual activity, personal response, and an act of the will. Once the conditions were present, in any of the theories we sketched out, the response of faith was immediate and coherent, the failure to believe somehow deficient, if not necessarily culpable. Today, however, the object of faith is seen less clearly and surrounded with all kinds of questions and uncertainties. What is it that we believe, if and when we believe? What are the human and social consequences of believing? What are the warrants for belief? Contemporary spirituality certainly concurs with those in the tradition who have stressed the intensely personal nature of the act of faith, that it is occasioned and nurtured by some kind of encounter, for Christians, with Jesus Christ. But what is contained in this encounter, what does it mean, and what is its relationship to the secular world in which everything actually occurs? The person of faith today, it would seem, is engaged in interpretation of the faith-encounter, not simply with accepting it. Of course, there are certainly those who retain the traditional "simple faith," but, with the exception of children, for whom it is both natural and appropriate, to believe without question may to some degree be imitating the ostrich. Faith no longer calls the shots for a totalizing explanation of reality, if it ever did. But faith does require a structured, nuanced embrace of the secular world. Theologically, even the secular world is God's world. Practically, the secular world is the world within which we live. The old religious adage "here we have no abiding city" used to mean that the world was relativized to some other world to come. To many people of faith today, certainly to the imprisoned Bonhoeffer, it means that the task of discipleship must be exercised in and for the world "come of age" in which, for a short time, we play our part.

If Christian theology traditionally took the role of context for granted in examining the tectonics of faith, it also did not pay attention to the complexity of the human person who was its subject. This is partially because the analysis of the act of faith took place in a highly abstract form where intellect and will, credibility and credentity shaped a set of reflections in which no actual, concrete human person was ever introduced as an example or a case study. It could not happen, because the philosophical discussion was conducted at a higher plane of universal principles where individual exemplars were simply not needed.[34] But a second reason why the human subject is absent from the traditional consideration of the act of faith is at least as important. Human subjectivity was not part of the philosophical equation. The debate was overwhelmingly deductive, producing universal principles that, of their nature, applied in all cases. The notion of the singular or the particular disrupting the philosophical conversation did not and could not occur. Only in the nineteenth century did the human psyche begin to be explored scientifically. Only then did the word "I" come to be problematized. And only then could we begin to ask about how the "I" affects the possibility of faith, or how the act of faith might change the "I." When I say, "I believe," I not only have to explore what is contained in the "belief" I claim to possess. I also need to be aware that the "I" that claims to believe needs also to be explored.

Today the act of faith is the acceptance of a claim upon us, one by means of which we interpret the secular world. Once we had believers and atheists. Today we have interpreters and attitudinizers. The latter take an attitude to the secular world as a given, either an unthematized acceptance of the world, warts and all, or a full or partial rejection of its values, coupled

---

[34] It would be possible to conduct philosophical discussions this way today. After all, much of the linguistic philosophy that held sway in places like Oxford in the 1960s and 1970s did exactly that.

perhaps with a determination to change it. Interpreters see the world, the secular world of today, in a more cosmic context. Interpreters inevitably bring a framework of understanding to the task, since otherwise there would be no means of interpretation. They may and do share much with those attitudinizers who recognize the ills of the secular world and wish to change it, but they will part company when asked why. Because of faith, the interpreter will put the whole of the world into a larger, cosmic picture and will, in a certain sense, love the whole. Even the less-than-lovable parts.

At the end of this chapter, then, we can express in preliminary fashion our understanding of the act of faith today. Whether a consciously Christian faith or not, the act of faith consists in the embrace of a loving Word/word that both calls and energizes the human subject to a life loving the world (discipleship). If the call to love seems somehow counterfactual, the life that follows the acceptance of the call makes more and more sense as it unfolds (here is the trope of consistency we encountered in the work of Rousselot). In traditional Christian theological terms, the personal encounter with Christ leads to a life loving the world for God. What makes the difference from previous ages is that the world we love for God is the secular world, the one where God seems unnecessary, the one in which we live, so much of the time, *etsi deus non daretur*.

■ ■ ■ ■ ■ ■   *Chapter Three*   ■ ■ ■ ■ ■ ■

Faith and Fiction

What Is Reading?

In the previous chapter we employed two terms drawn from the work of Wolfgang Iser to elucidate the difference between the act of faith in the past and the way in which the act of faith occurs today.[1] If one lives in an age or context of faith, where faith of a particular kind is, if not indisputable, at least the default position and that adopted by the vast majority of people, then whether one can make the act of faith or not is a matter of *attitude*. There it is, and we either buy it or we don't. The person of faith has adopted a positive attitude to the claim that God or the sacred is making upon him or her. The one who cannot make the act of faith simply says "no," in regret, or anger, or incomprehension. The unbeliever is deaf to the personal invitation to faith, probably because—in traditional terms—it doesn't seem credible and therefore the moral question of credentity simply does not arise. Today, while there are clearly those who find faith easy and many who see it as impossible, the interesting group, surely the majority, stand somewhere in between, not deaf to the call but not at all sure how, if at all, to respond. The act of faith is no longer one of attitude but now one of *interpretation*.

---

[1] Wolfgang Iser, *The Act of Reading: A Theory of Aesthetic Response* (Baltimore, MD: Johns Hopkins University Press, 1978).

Iser's distinction between attitude and interpretation clears the air of many misconceptions about the act of reading. There are so many prose texts that have only one acceptable meaning. For example, consider the problems that would arise if the wording on the label of your medication were written ambiguously. Or if the directions you were given to get to some previously unvisited location were composed too poetically. You might take the wrong dose, and you might very well show up extremely late for your appointment, if at all. Then there is a second group of texts that we can admit are written imaginatively and that seek to entertain rather than inform the reader, but that do not offer the reader much in the way of material that needs to be interpreted. Much but not all crime fiction falls into this category, as does everything in the "Harlequin Romance" school of fiction, most thrillers, and—dare we say it—*Fifty Shades of Grey* and *The Da Vinci Code*. Much erotic fiction avoids this category—think perhaps of *Justine* or *Lady Chatterley's Lover*—but all pornography almost defines it. One of the ways to tell the difference is to ask yourself how, if at all, the imagination and not merely the body is being stimulated. All of this and more is included by Iser under the heading of "light reading," a category that many of us value but he evidently does not. The third group of writings is where we find substantial fiction, and perhaps this is where the average bookstore gets its distinction between ordinary and "literary" fiction. The distinctive marker of fiction with literary value is that it requires the reader to engage with it imaginatively, relishing its suggestiveness and ambiguity, exploring and identifying meaning, at least meaning for the reading subject, and just enjoying the creative work of appropriating the text for oneself.

One of the central insights of Iser's *The Act of Reading* is that while the work itself sends out signals, they are not provided as a key or clue to the author's understanding of the text but in fact to stimulate the reader to a creative act in which meaning emerges from the interplay between the subjectivity of the reader and the objectivity of the text. Otherwise, of course, we would have only two options: either we would confine readers to puzzling out the one and only one meaning of the text, and that the one the author intended, or open interpretation to an anarchic frenzy of subjectivity in which absolutely any appropriation at all is of equal value and consequence as any other. The "aesthetic object" for Iser is not the text itself but the product of reading it. The aesthetic object emerges in the interplay between reader and text. This, then, is not simply "reader response theory," which might be where some (Terry Eagleton, for example[2]) would place Iser, but a particular version of it, which he names "aesthetic response" theory.

If the aesthetic object is a product of the act of reading a text and responding to its signals, where does the object actually reside? Not, obviously, inside the text itself, since it requires a reader, and not in the reader, since she or he requires a text. Instead, we have to think of the aesthetic object existing in "the space between" the text and the reader, evidently a virtual space. While this term is implicit throughout Iser's work it is most accessibly encountered in a recent book by Wendy Lesser. In *Why I Read: The Serious Pleasure of Books*,[3] Lesser considers many kinds of gaps left by authors in their texts, sometimes intentionally, sometimes accidentally, and sometimes forced upon them by narrow-minded editors. The clearest illustration in Lesser's discussion occurs in poetry where, she writes, "the kind of connection that is usually essential to our understanding of what is happening has been purposely removed."[4] So we are drawn by the mysterious and enigmatic character of poetry into a space left open for us in which to allow for

---

[2] Terry Eagleton, *Literary Theory: An Introduction* (Minneapolis: University of Minnesota Press, 1983), 78–84.

[3] Wendy Lesser, *Why I Read: The Serious Pleasure of Books* (New York: Farrar, Strauss & Giroux, 2014).

[4] Ibid., 42.

contact between what the text intends and what the reader encounters. The space between that interests us, then, is the space between the reader and the writer, the place and time where the creativity of the author and the imagination of the reader conspire together to illuminate the enigmas of human life. When the reader enters this space he or she is claimed by the text. Though Lesser chooses poetry, there is no particular reason why the insight could not apply equally well to fiction or, for that matter, to the visual arts. Is this not exactly what is happening when we look at Simberg's painting of the wounded angel?

In a more recent book,[5] Wolfgang Iser moves beyond his aesthetic response theory to a deeper exploration of the role of the reader in the process of creating fiction, which he names "literary anthropology." Providing a rare and extremely welcome concrete example, Iser offers the image of an actor who is playing the role of Hamlet. In order to do this effectively he must somehow "fade out his own reality." He cannot totally identify with Hamlet, not least because Hamlet as a character in a drama escapes total appropriation. The actor's self—body, feelings, and mind—act analogically to enable him to represent that which he is not. So, through his interpretation, what Hamlet *might be* comes into focus. Much the same is happening when we read a fiction, says Iser: "To imagine what has been stimulated by the 'as-if' entails placing our faculties at the disposal of an unreality and bestowing on it a semblance of reality in proportion to a reduction of our own reality."[6] In other words, when we bring a novel to life through reading a text, we have to subordinate our own reality to the process of treating the unreal *as-if* it were real. But what emerges is in part a product of the reader's own partially subordinated self.

---

[5] Wolfgang Iser, *The Fictive and the Imaginary: Charting Literary Anthropology* (Baltimore, MD: Johns Hopkins University Press, 1993).

[6] Ibid., 17.

The kind of process Iser is describing in the as-if nature of granting a measure of reality to what is unreal should, if we are alert, sound to us very much like game playing, and it comes as no surprise that the *Fictive and the Imaginary* reaches its climax with an analysis of reading as "play." The play that occurs, however, is not simply between the fictionalizing capacity of the reader and the text that has put forth signs for the reader to interpret. Iser introduces a third and vital element, which he calls "the imaginary." In the triadic play between text, fictionality, and the imaginary, the fictive gives form to the aesthetic object, but the imaginary gives life. At the same time, the tendency of the imaginary toward sheer fantasy is corralled by the fictive, while the fictive's potential subservience to the text is overcome by the liberating if not anarchic impulses of the imaginary. In a fascinating historical analysis, Iser shows how freeing the imaginary and the category of fiction from the status of illusion, deceit, or lies and bringing the imagination into focus as at least as important a human capacity as reason is owed in great measure to philosophy's recognition that it too relies to some degree on fiction. Not coincidentally, the world of Locke, Hume, and Kant is also the world in which the novel begins to achieve prominence.

Iser's often extremely abstract and highly technical discussion comes in the end to an important conclusion. Human beings, he argues, can never be in full possession of themselves, though they would like to be. We are ourselves, but we do not have ourselves. This is where literature reveals its critical importance, because it offers us what Iser calls "staging." In literature, "the impossibility of being present to ourselves becomes our possibility to play ourselves out to a fullness that knows no bounds." "If the plasticity of human nature . . . allows limitless human self-cultivation," he continues, then "literature becomes a panorama of what is possible." And he adds, in a rare comment of theological mien: "To monitor changing manifestations of self-fashioning, and yet not coincide with any of them, makes the interminable staging of ourselves appear as the postponement of the end."[7] In the human person there is the duality of what we are and what we are not, though what we are is not finally accessible to us and what we might be is always only possibility. But literature allows us "an ecstatic life" in which we can be anything we want to be while simultaneously reminding us of the stable self that we are even as we explore "the possibilities of our otherness." So, "precisely because cognitive discourse cannot capture the duality adequately, we have literature."[8]

What Is Reading For?

If Wolfgang Iser makes a strong case for reading as a principal means by which the human imagination is stimulated and satisfied, and offers a salutary correction to overemphasis upon ratiocination, he does not link his view to any overarching moral purpose. A theoretician, perhaps, is unlikely to see that as important, in written work if not in actual life. But if Iser's responsibility is to explain what is going on in the space between the reader and the text at an altitude that does not allow for ethical considerations, it is nevertheless true that his elitist taxonomy of fiction hints at a larger or deeper purpose. Iser frequently dismisses "light reading" as that which doesn't merit a second look. The kind of reading we all might do at times for sheer entertainment, thrillers, romances, detective fiction, is easily dismissed. This reading, because it has no ambiguity, demands nothing of its reader. We simply "go with the flow," trying to solve the puzzle or enjoying the suspense, but in no way does the text "read us." The act of reading *worthy* fiction, by contrast, engages us in a process that may change or amplify our sense of our human possibilities. But it is the

[7] Ibid., 297.
[8] Ibid., 303.

range of possibility, not any particular direction it might take, that he leaves us with.

Mark Edmundson, by contrast, a teacher rather than a literary theorist, is convinced of the critical moral significance of reading. In a series of books[9] Edmundson charts the struggle in the contemporary world between "self" and "soul" (his words) and makes an extended impassioned plea for reading. An agnostic himself, Edmundson believes that the right place to begin all teaching in the humanities is with religion, since even if the subject matter of the course is not religion, religion is likely to figure substantially in what he calls his students' "final narratives." The "final narrative" is "the ultimate set of terms that we use to confer value on experience," which tells us something about what each of us holds as "ultimate terms of commitment, the point beyond which argument and analysis are unlikely to go, at least very quickly."[10] Claiming that his approach goes back at least to Socrates, Edmundson says that "posing the question of religion and the good life allows students to become articulate about who and what they are," and he admits that this implies a value judgment, "that the most consequential questions for an individual life . . . are related to questions of faith."[11] Edmundson eventually comes clean that his project "is a form of humanism," defined in this way: "Humanism is the belief that it is possible for some of us, and maybe more than some, to use secular writing as the preeminent means for shaping our lives."[12]

In Edmundson's undergraduate classroom students are not asked to explore literary theory but to approach the reading of

[9] Especially Mark Edmundson, *Why Read?* (New York: Bloomsbury, 2004); *Why Teach? In Defense of a Real Education* (New York: Bloomsbury, 2013); and *Self and Soul: A Defense of Ideals* (Cambridge, MA: Harvard University Press, 2015).

[10] Edmundson, *Why Read?*, 26.

[11] Ibid., 27.

[12] Ibid., 86.

a text with a question like, "Can this book help shape my life?" So while there is undoubtedly a process of interpretation at work in confronting great literature, it is something like Schopenhauer's conviction that the question works of art raise is simply, "What is life?" and that "every successful work of art answers this question in its own way with perfect correctness."[13] In a passage that Wolfgang Iser would undoubtedly approve of, Edmundson quotes Milan Kundera's view that novels are populated by "experimental selves," that is, "persons whom we might become," and that the novelist puts them out there to see what readers will make of them. As Kundera puts it, "The world of one single Truth and the relative, ambiguous world of the novel are molded of entirely different substances. Totalitarian Truth excludes relativity, doubt, questioning; it can never accommodate what I would call *the spirit of the novel*."[14] Edmundson's attention to his students' "final narratives" differs from traditional religious formulations of ultimate commitments in one important respect that presses us to ask if the pedagogical process of acquiring wisdom that he evidently favors indeed has any teleology. Does reading give life a direction, a goal, or is it all in the process? Following the ironist Richard Rorty, Edmundson believes that the final narrative is anything but final and that, indeed, the process of reading and being read by what we read is all part of the dynamism of an ever-changing and provisional final narrative. The question is whether democratic openness about visions of the good life is itself ultimate or if there are substantive values to be uncovered in the process of reading. Returning to Edmundson's humanism, is secular fiction a "preeminent means" by which some of us at least may shape our lives because the process is therapeutic, or because it uncovers values that may, indeed, escape ironic detachment?

[13] Quoted in ibid., 61.
[14] Quoted in ibid., 68.

That Edmundson believes reading can shape our lives in substantial ways becomes quite apparent in his 2015 book, *Self and Soul*. Subtitled *A Defense of Ideals*, this work explores the virtues of courage and compassion and the search for truth by examining the figures of the hero, the saint, and the thinker against the background of what he calls "the triumph of self" in the modern world. While the canvas here is larger than that in his earlier book, Edmundson sees literature as a possible way to overcome the unhealthy focus on the self and its satisfactions and to restore attention to ideals. His *bêtes noires* in the decline of ideals and the triumph of the self are Shakespeare (a surprise to some, perhaps many) and Sigmund Freud (less surprising). His literary saviors are Blake and Shelley, with longing backward looks to Emerson and Thoreau. And the means by which they offer salvation, albeit secular, is through creativity and the work of the imagination.

One of the more striking conclusions we can draw from reading Edmundson is that he has a passionate commitment to the importance of reading for the emergence of a humane self, while suggesting no particular direction in which one must move in order to develop. The process of reading may in itself make us better people, or it may be that in the process of reading we encounter values that propose to us a better way to be—both seem to be at work in Edmundson's books—but in either case the conclusions that will follow are unrestrictedly pluralistic. He quotes Allan Bloom favorably: "Liberal education does put everything at risk and requires students who are willing to risk everything."[15] We need to become aware of our own ignorance and we need to be unendingly willing to revise our final narratives. In *Self and Soul* Edmundson seems, on the one hand, to want to hark back to the classic ideals of the hero, the saint, and the thinker, but he also wants to propose a new ideal of the creative imagination. There is much more fluidity

[15] Ibid., 32.

—Iser would call it "plasticity"—in the creative work of the imagination than in the restoration of the heroic obsession with glory, the way of self-abnegation, or the asceticism of the thinker. But all, perhaps, move us toward ethics.

Whether reading is in fact an ethical act, and what it would mean to talk about "the ethics of reading," is by no means a simple question to answer. J. Hillis Miller confronted this question at the outset of a short book exploring how writers read and reread their own work: "Does it mean a mode of ethics or of ethical action generated by reading, deriving from it, or does it mean an ethics intrinsic to reading, remaining within it?"[16] His close attention to passages from the writing of Immanuel Kant, Paul de Man, George Eliot, Anthony Trollope, and Henry James lead him to the latter conclusion. There is something about the process of reading, at least when it is a matter of writers encountering their own work, for which Miller believes the word "ethics" is appropriate. But what is ethical is not the text itself, nor inhering mysteriously in the text, but the "ethical law" of which the text is an illustration but whose full reality cannot be encountered beyond the illustrations.[17] In what are hopefully simpler words than those of Miller in this particularly densely argued book, the distinction here is between laws and the law as such. Kant's categorical imperative may be law, but there is nowhere you can find it other than in how it dictates—according to Kant—what course of action we should choose in any particular concrete situation. In this sense, the law is primary but does not actually exist. To be ethical is to accept "the law," but this only shows itself in my obedience to particular laws or, indeed, in my unwillingness to obey.

---

[16] J. Hillis Miller, *The Ethics of Reading: Kant, de Man, Eliot, Trollope, James, and Benjamin* (New York: Columbia University Press, 1987), 1.

[17] The attentive reader might note here some echoes of Ockham's nominalism.

The importance of this somewhat arcane distinction is clearest in Miller's discussion of Henry James's preface to the New York edition of *The Golden Bowl*.[18] In the interest of both clarity and brevity we will set aside Miller's exposition, though not his insight, and go straight to James's own words, since Miller seems more under the influence of James's strangled syntax than is helpful. In this preface James is examining the relationship between the author and the novels which, in this case, *he* wrote in the past and which he is now rereading for purposes of criticism. There are two elements of this preface that are particularly germane to our trying to understand what is going on in the act of reading: one that pertains to questions of the meaning of the text and one that addresses what it is in and through the text that incites the reader's response. Both James and Miller following him are concerned with how the writer of a text reads or rereads the text he or she once wrote, but our hunch (and indeed Miller's[19]) is that the analysis will not be significantly different for the general reader.

For James, the significance of the novel does not lie in the story, not even in the characters, but in the "matter" (his word) that lies behind the text. The author's work consists in creating a narrative that somehow gives expression to the "matter" without ever surfacing it. The reader's (and writer's) relationship to the matter is accessed through the story, both plot and character, while it is never entirely uncovered. This "matter," which is what in the end the story is actually *about*, is never finally clear to writer or reader. The story itself is a means, a mode of access to the ever-mysterious and unattainable matter. The author will succeed by presenting the story in such a way that the reader's imagination is, dare we say, *inspired* to go beyond the surface to access the matter, probably without ever

---

[18] Miller, *The Ethics of Reading*, 101–22. For the text of James's preface, see Henry James, *Literary Criticism* (New York: The Library of America, 1984), 1322–41.

[19] Miller, *The Ethics of Reading*, 121.

realizing that this is happening. To illustrate this, note the concern Henry James expressed about the illustrations to *The Golden Bowl* that graced the New York edition. He and his photographer went to great pains *not* to illustrate the story at all, not to provide likenesses of the characters in the story or illustrations of incidents. Because they would fix the reader's attention on the surface of plot and character, they would hinder careful reading, and because they would inevitably reflect the author's conceptions, they would frustrate the creativity of the reader. As James puts it, the author's "own garden . . . remains one thing, and the garden he has prompted the cultivation of at other hands becomes quite another."[20] What makes the illustrations valuable is that they "seek the way, which they have happily found, I think, not to keep, or to pretend to keep, anything like dramatic step with their suggestive matter."[21] In other words, they do not illustrate the narrative, but they do, if wisely chosen, somehow refer to the matter of the story.

Henry James would be uncomfortable with questions about the meaning of his fictions. His stories are "representations," and his work is quite deliberately done to defuse questions about its significance. Not only does Henry James the author never appear as the narrator of his fictions; the narrator he chooses almost never does anything other than report on the characters in the tale, their doings, and, especially, their conversations. By means of this consistent authorial device, James believes that "the whole business—that is, as I say, its effective interest—[is] enriched *by the way*." Anything would be better, he continues, "for the process and the effect of representation, my irrepressible ideal—than the mere muffled majesty of irresponsible 'authorship.'"[22]

---

[20] James, *Literary Criticism*, 1326.

[21] Ibid., 1327.

[22] Ibid., 1322–23.

The second issue of particular moment for us is James's use of the term "the absolute" to designate that which we may encounter in reading or rereading the text, not indeed for its apparently religious resonances, but in fact because he seems not to intend to invoke the category of transcendence at all. James reaches this point in his close examination of the notion of revision, important of course because for the New York edition of his works he made significant changes to many of the novels and he perhaps felt the need to justify them. He was, he says, always opposed to rewriting, because once you start tinkering with the building it "might let one in, as the phrase is, for expensive renovations."[23] He eventually realized, however, that revision literally does not mean "rewriting" but "re-reading," and so in a rare sophistical moment he excuses the many changes in the New York edition as "these rigid conditions of re-perusal, registered."[24] This "infinitely interesting and amusing *act* of re-appropriation" with its exhilarating freedom seems to him "almost as enlivening, or at least momentous, as, to a philosophic mind, a sudden large apprehension of the Absolute." "What could be more delightful," he adds, "than to enjoy a sense of the absolute in such easy conditions?"[25]

What exactly James means by invoking the absolute at this point in his argument is unclear, but it must have something to do with the mysterious "matter" of the fiction. In the first place, he suggests that the experience of reappropriating his own earlier writings is analogous, not identical, to the philosopher's apprehension of "the Absolute." But he goes on, notably abandoning the uppercase "A" for the woollier notion of "the absolute," to seem to claim to be enjoying this absolute in the act of reappropriation. Evidently, he is not interested in claiming contact with "God" or "the transcendent" or even "the

---

[23] Ibid., 1331.
[24] Ibid., 1332.
[25] Ibid., 1330.

Absolute." But the analogy of absolute to Absolute seems to depend on an unspoken element of identity, namely, that neither the Absolute nor the absolute, while it is apprehended or sensed, is ever actually possessed. Nor, equally important, is it arrived at by the exercise of reason. Reason or the imagination can perhaps prepare the ground, but the A/absolute, if it has any reality at all, cannot be commanded. It can only be approached through that which it is not, perhaps philosophical reasoning, perhaps writing, perhaps (re)reading. What is so exciting for James in the act of reappropriation is surely the renewed encounter with the matter of the fiction. But the matter is quite ungraspable. As Wendy Lesser says in her own version of the Jamesian conundrum, using the category of truth, "I will invoke the notion often, and yet I will not be able to define it for you, except by example."[26]

When we ask what reading fiction is for, it is not too jejune to answer simply, "for pleasure." If we did not derive pleasure from fiction, why would any of us do it? Writing about the pleasures of reading, it is unusual to encounter an author who does not distinguish, whatever the terms used, between light and serious fiction. This is not the same division as that between bad and good writing. There are plenty of fine examples of writing in the distinctly nonelitist categories of crime fiction or comic novels, and God knows there are aspirants to serious fiction who achieve only the turgid or the plainly boring. Light and serious fiction are indeed different, and Iser's distinction between books to which we simply must take an attitude and those which demand interpretation may be a good way to go. Both types of writing draw a reader in search of pleasure and retain the reader's attention only when pleasure is provided. One person cannot finish a book that another treasures, and while we can analyze why until the cows come home, the truth is that the first is not deriving pleasure and the second undoubtedly is.

[26] Lesser, *Why I Read*, 8.

To say that all good writing gives pleasure to its readers does not at all mean that there is only one kind of pleasure to be derived from good writing, and here we come to what counts. The serious reader is not the one who casts aside Mickey Spillane and will read only Dostoevsky, but the one who can enjoy the simple pleasures of thrillers, sci-fi, horror, or even romance but who is also in search of the more sophisticated pleasures that require considerably more application from the reader. Serious fiction is not just about itself, and reading it is not just about taking it at its surface level. The "more" that it is a vehicle for is the "matter" that so occupies Henry James's attention, or the absolute, if not the Absolute, that may be glimpsed in careful reading. If you read a classic detective fiction novel of high caliber—say a work of Ngaio Marsh or Margery Allingham—and someone asks you what it was about, you will tell the story. But if having just finished *The Brothers Karamazov* and getting the same question, you tell your questioner that it is a mystery about who murdered Fyodor Karamazov, you sadly missed the point. That is surely the form of the novel, but it is most definitely not the matter. And if you really think that this is what the novel is about, then you missed out on a great deal of pleasure available at a higher level.

While it is possible to sound extraordinarily elitist in ascribing higher or deeper levels of pleasure to more "serious" fiction, one can also avoid this pitfall by linking the pleasures of more challenging reading to the question of ethics, not now in the sense stressed by J. Hillis Miller, but in the more customary usage of the term. The broadest meaning of ethics, something akin to the thinking of Mark Edmundson, is well-expressed by Wayne Booth as "a belief that a given way of reading, or a given kind of literature, is what will do us most good."[27] For

---

[27] Wayne C. Booth, *The Company We Keep: An Ethics of Fiction* (Berkeley: University of California Press, 1988), 5.

Booth and for most readers, ethical reading and hence ethical criticism is the norm. There is no way to stand outside reading in order to prove what is going on in reading, but Booth (and surely Edmundson) believes "that fictions are the most powerful of all the architects of our souls and societies."[28] Nevertheless, Booth warns against employing the term "ethical" erroneously, "to suggest an interest only in judging stories and their effects on readers." There is also "the ethics *of* readers—their responsibilities *to* stories."[29] Utilizing the title of his book to link together the many senses of "ethical" and to exclude some that are not appropriate, Booth understands the books we read to be in some sense our friends, our conversation partners, and asks: "What kind of company are we keeping as we read or listen? What kind of company have we kept?"[30]

The ethics of fiction, whether that of writing or reading, has nothing in itself to do with the moral content of the narrative. "To grasp morality as a great novelist understands it," writes Terry Eagleton, "is to see it as an intricately woven texture of nuances, qualities and fine gradations." Of course, he goes on, "novels convey moral truths, though not in the sense that Oral Roberts or Ian Paisley would recognize."[31] As James insisted and Booth has implied, the need for both writer and reader is to be honest. The writer crafts a fiction whose integrity depends on its faithfulness to the matter it somehow but never perfectly represents and reveals. The reader, and James rereading his own fiction, must both be open to the claim the narrative is making and yet retain a critical awareness of its effect. The story itself is important but so also is the honesty of the author and the reader alike. It is entirely possible, however, to

[28] Ibid., 39.
[29] Ibid., 9.
[30] Ibid., 10.
[31] Terry Eagleton, *After Theory* (New York: Basic Books, 2003), 144.

encounter fictions whose characters or situations might be considered immoral and yet conclude that the work itself is ethically conducted and has a positive impact on the reader. Equally, one can certainly read fictions whose characters and situations are impeccably moral while suspecting that the author is just out to make money, knowing that the reader finds such stories stultifying, boring, self-indulgent, or just plain dishonest, and so could never say that they "will do us most good." Indeed, if we spend our lives in this kind of bad company, even if the subject matter is itself ethically sound, we will descend to the level of the texts, just as surely as if our real-life friends are empty-headed pleasure seekers, we will almost certainly become such ourselves. Let's give Henry James the last word here:

> But on all the ground to which the pretension of performance by a series of exquisite laws may apply there reigns one sovereign truth—which decrees that, as art is nothing if not exemplary, care nothing if not active, finish nothing if not consistent, the proved error is the base apologetic deed, the helpless regret is the barren commentary, and "connexions" are employable for finer purposes than mere gaping contrition.[32]

Faithful Reading and Reading Faith

Reading is a human act saturated in mystery. Even looked at mechanically, the process by which the brain moves from marks on a page to images in the mind is a thing of wonder. When a child begins to read, this is not simply one more sign of intellectual development, since children in nonliterate cultures grow into perfectly capable and admirable human beings possessed of skills and wisdom that "readers" may not have at all. Something marvelous, something qualitatively different

---

[32] James, *Literary Criticism*, 1341.

happens when we acquire the skill of reading. It is most definitely not a natural activity and, as we all of us have had occasion to notice, once we acquire the skill of reading, reading acquires us. So long as a text is in our own language, when our eyes alight on it, we cannot not read it. The capacity to read actually changes the brain permanently. Short of brain disease, there is no going back.

Once we look beyond the mere mechanics to the substance contained in the act of reading, as we have been doing in this chapter, we plunge into even murkier waters. We know, of course, that when we read a novel we somehow enter into a world conjured up by the author but not simply determined by him or her. The "meaning" of the fiction, if we can use that term, is decided neither by the author nor by the reader but rather negotiated in the space between the reader and the text, a "meaning" that has at an earlier stage been produced in the always imperfect and inconclusive telling of the story that occurs between the author and the finished (if it is ever finished) text. And if we are clear that the fundamental purpose of reading fiction is pleasure, the pleasure is enabled by the actual act of reading, but for the vast majority of readers the pleasure obtained is not identical to the act of reading but resides in whatever it is that the act of reading transmits from the text to the reader's sensibility. The "whatever it is" that the reader receives in the act of reading involves some measure of intellectual activity, usually some emotional response, and some instigation of imaginative juices, but it is not identical to any or all of these three combined. The proportion of imagination, emotion, and intellect will certainly vary depending on the particular work of fiction, and if the reading is successful—that is, if it indeed produces sufficient pleasure—then we are still left with the question, what *kind* of pleasure is it that we receive? And if we determine, as we well might, that it is *aesthetic* pleasure, we only push our question one step further. For what, indeed, *is* "aesthetic pleasure"?

   This is an appropriate point to ask ourselves in a preliminary way about some of the similarities and differences between the act of faith and the act of reading. While it would
be a mistake to think of these two acts as ordered to the same
end, since "faith" and "pleasure," though not absolute contrar-
ies, are surely different, there are things to be said about the
role of the author, about textual matters and about the mysterious exchange in the space between the text and the human
subject. There are certainly some structural parallels, and they
may be sufficient in number to lead to a suspicion that the two
activities may have more in common than is typically thought.
And it is not inconceivable that when we pursue just what the
pleasure of reading is, we may find that the reach toward an
imaginative grasp of the whole is not so different from the act
of faith as we might have imagined.

   At the source of the act of faith in the Christian tradition
there is a person whom the believer first encounters through
the text of Scripture. Within the Christian tradition that person
encountered is Jesus Christ, and the relationship that ensues
for the person of faith is a dynamic one, fueled by prayer and
by periodic recourse to Scripture. Through prayer, the relationship grows in depth and intensity, always somehow under the
control of the form contained in Scripture, above all in the
gospels, but always possessing a personal dimension that reflects in part the personality and historical context of the person of faith. So there is a subjective dimension. It is *my* act of
faith and not yours. And there is an objective dimension. My
act of faith and yours are both acts of faith in the person of
Jesus Christ as the revelation of God in history. But the content
of the act of faith occurs and is further determined in the space
between the faithful subject and the text that is the principal
vehicle of transmission of the person who is the object of faith.[33]

---

[33] For Catholics, the living tradition of the church as the transhistorical
communion of saints is a secondary vehicle, always consistent with and so
dependent on the primary witness of Scripture.

In this space between, the person of faith encounters Christ and the relationship between the two grows over time. To that extent, faith is entirely individual. But because the space between is to a degree controlled by the form of the text, there is also a communal dimension to the act of faith. It is always my own, and it is also always shaped by the text that the community of faith asserts as its primary witness to the reality of God's saving grace in Jesus Christ.

When we describe the structure of the act of faith as the encounter with a person in the space between the believer and the text, it is obvious that there are significant structural parallels to the act of reading fiction. The reader of fiction who wishes to obtain the maximum pleasure must practice disciplined attention to the text and simultaneously abandon self to the text. The reader must read carefully and must let the signs left in the text by the author work their magic on him or her, producing a vision of a world and characters within it that engage, entrance, and instruct. Moreover, as we read and especially as we reread the work of fiction, we typically report finding "more and more" in the text. Our appreciation for the characters grows in rereading, or we would not be rereading at all. Even on a first reading the fiction grows in depth in our minds as we work in the space between. Perhaps this is what Vladimir Nabokov meant by his typically gnomic utterance that "curiously enough, one cannot read a book; one can only reread it." A good reader, he added, "a major reader, an active and creative reader is a re-reader."[34] All good readers are at one and the same time absorbing and questioning the text, letting the text work on them while they also work on the text.

If we can identify structural parallels between the act of faith and the act of reading, it is no less true that there are significant

---

[34] Vladimir Nabokov, "Good Readers and Good Writers," *Lectures on Literature* (New York: Harcourt, 2002), 1–9. The text of this introductory essay is available online: https://thefloatinglibrary.com/2009/08/09/good-readers -and-good-writers-vladimir-nabokov/.

differences. Most obviously, the act of faith is in one person, however much we understand the faith relationship to be dynamic, while the act of reading, though it is at any one time dealing with only one fiction, of its nature moves on from one story to another. If people of faith decide that they have had enough of Jesus and decide to move on to Krishna or Zoroaster, the faith simply dissolves. It isn't faith unless it practices fidelity, though the depth or character of the faith may change over time. And if readers come to the conclusion that one book is so perfect that they need never move on to another but will simply reread this one over and over again, then we might be inclined to accuse them of narrow-minded literary fundamentalism and account them "not serious readers." The commitment to one and one only is a necessity for religious faith but a fundamental failing for the reader of fiction. Openness to sheer variety among a plurality of options is the lifeblood of the reader but death to religious belief. This is not to say, however, that religious commitment to one particular story cannot be possessed sufficiently generously to allow for the value of others.

A second consideration follows from observing the different senses of faithfulness in faith and reading. Readers look for truthful texts and make the effort to read them honestly, but there is no sense that one text holds the key and that others must be interpreted in its light. On the contrary, however, people of faith in the Christian tradition take Jesus Christ to be the hermeneutical principle by which all aspects of reality must be measured. Christian faith is incarnational and Christocentric, which means that the embodied and indeed human God is the point of access to the riches of faith. To make a similar claim for *Moby Dick* or *Anna Karenina* would be blasphemy to a faith perspective and utter stupidity to readers, even to those like Mark Edmundson who believe "that it is possible for some of us, and maybe more than some, to use secular writing as the preeminent means for shaping our lives."

The challenge to the person of faith is consequently to find ways in which to affirm pluralism and ambiguity, contemporary virtues that do not sit easily with traditional faith. The challenge to the secular reader is to recognize limits to *which* texts may help shape our lives for the better and which not.

A further difference might lie in what we can call the eschatological perspective of life-shaping through secular writing and life-shaping through the gospel. The former eschews all teleology; the latter embraces it. If secular readers find themselves one day in heaven, surrounded by their favorite books and all those they meant to read but didn't, their surprise will only be exceeded by their delight. But their beliefs in the here and now conform to the well-worn adage, "so many books, so little time." The comedy of reading for pleasure is enclosed within the tragedy of its inevitable interruption. The believer, who sees in Christ's resurrection the promise of life with God forever, will not be surprised if it does not happen but will just not be. Of course, the believer who is also a reader, and the category is a very large one, will include in eschatological hope the fervent wish that books will not meet the fate of marriage. Jesus tells the Pharisees that "in the resurrection they neither marry nor are given in marriage, but are like angels in heaven" (Matt 22:30; RSV). Bookish believers will be eager to find that angels are avid readers.

If so far in this chapter we have focused on the necessity for faithful reading, it is time to turn our attention to a few thoughts about "reading faith." Faithful reading is only another term for the integrity of purpose on the part of author and reader alike that goes by the name of the ethics of reading. The term "reading faith" is far less transparent. To read faith will mean to apply the same kinds of virtuous practices involved in the act of reading, openness and disciplined critique, to the phenomenon of faith, to faith as a text, or more perhaps as an almost infinite number of texts, since there is no such thing as faith that is not instantiated as this person's faith or that person's faith. The way forward may very well be to ask if there is such a thing as the ethics of faith and if so, how it can be construed. To do so is to enter difficult terrain where we may need to use unfamiliar and challenging concepts. If we see God as the author or instigator of the (con)text in which faith can occur, must we ask about divine integrity? And as we explore the conditions of the believer who has responded to the text of faith, shall we find ourselves judging what is good or bad faith, weak or strong faith, faith that is false or true? And is it possible to take on such daunting tasks with appropriate humility?

As it happens, the ethics of faith is the subject of one of the greatest books in the Hebrew Bible, the book of Job.[35] Job, the man of perfect integrity, finds himself subjected to terrible suffering at the hands of God in a world in which suffering is supposed only to be a sign of punishment for sin. Whether we focus on the ancient myth enshrined in the first two chapters, in which Job is the object of a bet between God and his avenging angel, Satan, or on the lengthy debate between Job and his "friends," which centers on the question of innocent suffering, the ethical questions are clear. Is God behaving with integrity when he uses Job in a bet with Satan? Is Job behaving with integrity when he accepts the suffering from God with patient resignation? Is Job's argument in the debate with his friends both ethical and faithful? Is the God who eventually claims at length to be the author of all that is (where were you when I created the universe?) treating Job ethically? When Job bows to God's power, who has the greater integrity? Finally and most important, when we read the story, either as humanists or believers, how do our openness to the text and our respon-

---

[35] For an introductory set of remarks on the book of Job as a source for a postmodern image of God, see Paul Lakeland, *Postmodernity: Christian Identity in a Fragmented Age* (Minneapolis: Fortress Press, 1997), 96–98.

sibility to critical awareness coincide or collide? Is it different for the secular person and the believer?

The secular reader encountering the book of Job will inevitably treat it as a parable illustrating the intellectual and emotional impossibility of believing with integrity. God is a tyrant in the opening myth, a bully at the end of the debate. Job is blindly committed to a capricious God in the myth, while in the debate his honest questioning is abandoned in favor of a cringing obeisance to a God who allows him no voice at all. The only ethical posture in the entire poem is in Job's defiance, and it is temporary. The terminus of Job's faith lies in abandoning his trust in his intellect in favor of divine power, only to be rewarded with a profusion of worldly goods and comforts. To the secular reader, the book of Job is a great work, a sublime exercise of the ethics of fiction that removes from the reader any possibility of reading with integrity and arriving at an ethics of belief.

Like the secular reader, the believer comes from a context that to a degree predetermines the outcome of the reading. We are all to some extent products of our upbringing and environment. But unlike the more secular individual, the believer will push on through the difficult surface of the text to a point at which an ethics of belief emerges, even perhaps strengthened by reading Job. In James's terms, the believer's reading gets closer to "the matter" of the text, though never in such a way that the full extent of the matter is revealed. What the secular reader correctly identifies as inadequate reasons to believe are similarly categorized by the believer. There is no integrity in accepting a purely capricious God. There is no truth to the claim that God causes suffering only to the wicked and blesses the good person with abundant riches. There is no honor in abandoning one's intellectual and moral integrity to a simple show of divine power. But the believer knows that the ethics of faith, like the ethics of reading, goes beyond the surface meaning of the text to the matter whose ultimacy is shrouded in mystery. When Job bows to God it is not subjection to power but rather to mystery. Even if the God of the book of Job is unethical, the ethics of faith goes beyond the fiction to the mysterious matter to which it attests, the believer's conviction that faith "is what will do us most good."

So What about the Imagination?

Throughout these first chapters we have seen considerable convergence between the ways in which a person embraces faith in the Christian God and the ways in which a serious reader opens herself or himself to the "matter" of the book that she or he is reading. In Aquinas and Rousselot, on the one hand, and in Coleridge and Henry James, on the other, we encounter theories of how the mystery or the "matter" (much the same) both illuminate the perspective of the believing or reading subject and at the same time elude full comprehension. The matter of serious fiction may seem to be comprehensible in principle, since it remains solely a finite phenomenon, but since neither the reader *nor the author* actually possesses it fully and can articulate it, there may be reason to toy with preferring the word "mystery" even to describe this. The matter of religion is more securely located in the realm of the transcendent, but the act of faith occurs within the finite realm and for this reason if for no other is quite similar to the reach of the reader toward the matter lying behind the text.

Both the act of faith and the act of reading are works of the imagination, in the sense in which Coleridge uses the term to distinguish it from "mere fancy." Of course, reading and faith are themselves activities in which fancy plays a role. Reading requires us to pick up all sorts of signals from the author and to allow the words to translate into images in our minds, even to embellish sometimes the details with which we have been provided. When we see a movie based on a book we have read we may find ourselves saying, "Oh, I didn't think of the hero looking quite like that!" This is not a judgment on how the part was cast or what the costume designer chose but a testament to the powers of our fancy. The act of faith is even more dependent on fancy, since the infinite God of mystery escapes all possible human images and yet we cannot talk about or talk to God without employing exactly those anthropomorphisms that we know mean, in the end, absolutely nothing. God's decision for incarnation saves Christianity from total silence, but the task of relating what we say about Jesus Christ to the mystery of God remains challenging, even daunting.

While it is entirely unproblematic to declare that reading is an act of the imagination, to call faith "an act of the imagination" raises many more questions for at least some believers. Perhaps religious believers can be led to see that faith is an imaginative activity, in the sense in which Coleridge describes it, by starting from the analysis of the act of reading. It is not, of course, an act of fancy, but how many would know or appreciate a distinction like that of Coleridge is hard to say. Coleridge, at any rate, is content to describe the imagination in religious terms as "the living power and prime agent of all human perception" and as "a repetition in the finite mind of the eternal act of creation in the infinite I AM." This "primary" imagination requires the "secondary" component, which is the work of the creative artist bringing the reader into contact with the "eternal act of creation" through something—the work of art—which is not divine creation but which points to and in some way mediates it to the reader.

The similarities between faith and reading are informative, even substantial. The creative artist, in particular but by no means exclusively the writer of prose fiction, sets out to tell a story that, if the author is successful, is somehow a conduit for the reader to grasp something that lies beyond the story, in the realm of the matter/mystery. As we saw earlier in examining Wolfgang Iser's approach to literature, the "aesthetic object" is not the text itself but the product of reading it, so that it emerges in the interplay between reader and text. When we turn to consider faith, there is no human "author" of the moment in which the believer makes the act of faith. God, we might reasonably say, is the author of the scenario, the created world, in which the act of faith necessarily takes place. But the act of faith itself is a free act of the will, informed by reason, in which the person says yes to a vision of the whole with which he or she has been presented. Rousselot would concur in considering this act an act of love. But while as an act of faith it can achieve certitude, its object can never be fully grasped, just as the "matter" of the work of fiction escapes full comprehension by either writer or reader. What "God" is and what "the meaning of the whole" is can never be finally accessible to the finite mind, though each in its own way may provide direction and meaning for the whole of a human life. Here at the end of part 1 of this book we come full circle to Aquinas, whose thought, of course, lies behind that of Rousselot. In responding to the question, "Whether the object of faith is something complex, by way of a proposition?" (II-II), Aquinas concludes that "the act of the faithful does not aim at the word as such, but at the matter [*rem*]."[36] Though, of course, in this life of faith we never attain the full knowledge of God that will be our reward in the Beatific Vision.

It seems, then, that it is entirely appropriate to understand faith as an act of the imagination, even perhaps simply as "imagination." It is, to quote Edgar Allan Poe one more time, "possibly, in man, a lesser degree of the creative power in God." Faith, as Aquinas certainly believed, is not in this or that, though this or that can be believed in the context of belief in God as the ground of all knowledge and all knowing. Faith

---

[36] Q. 1, a. 2, ad 2. Quoted in Christoph Theobald's translation in *The Legacy of Vatican II*, ed. Massimo Faggioli and Andrea Vicini (New York: Paulist Press, 2015), 42. The Latin text reads: *Actus autem credentis non terminatur ad enuntiabile, sed ad rem.*

is then a fundamental attitude to ourselves and the world around us, because it is belief in the First Truth that grounds all we can know and all our knowing.

There is one last question before we conclude this chapter, this one occasioned by returning to Bonhoeffer and to the working understanding of faith today. How can we talk about "certitude"? Must we not consider faith, this side of the Beatific Vision, to be inevitably provisional? The answer to this begins to lay bare the poverty of contemporary understandings of faith, which are for the most part versions of belief in some particular thing, even some particular God considered as an object. In such a case faith is inevitably provisional, particularly since this kind of God will almost certainly disappoint us as we inspect the extent of pain, suffering, and plain old evil at work in our world, even sometimes through the agency of so-called believers. But if we can go along with Aquinas, Rousselot, and even Coleridge and perceive faith as a fundamental attitude to all that is as pure gift, gift which, if it does not necessarily imply for all of us a giver, certainly recognizes that we are not ourselves the producers of that from which we benefit, then this kind of faith—perhaps possessed equally by believers and more secular human beings—might, this side of the pure nihilism of Dostoevsky's *Underground Man*, both insulate us from being overcome by the power of evil and unite us in the struggle against the same power.

In this struggle, fiction can be enormously helpful in a number of ways that we will consider as we proceed through the remaining chapters, though one way in particular stands out, namely, in the rehabilitation of the wounded imaginations of our present day. The incapacity to grasp any sense of transcendence is simply a failure of imagination, one that has all but emptied the churches and that goes a long way toward explaining the anomie of our world. The churches have opted for moralizing in the guise of preaching, paying less and less attention to the celebration of mystery in the liturgy and the urgency to heal the pain of the world that is incumbent upon the eucharistic community. While those who abandon religious practice often do so in search of a sense of the meaning of the whole that they feel traditional religion has failed to provide, once they step outside all overt religion, the search becomes harder, even as it may be more authentic. The meaning of the whole, or what we used to call metaphysics, is not culturally fashionable and can be pursued in the secular world, if at all, only in the immensely difficult terrain of an individual quest. In part 2 of this book we turn to the question of the relationship between faith, metaphysics, and fiction.

Part Two ■

Religion and Literature

■ ■ ■ ■ ■ ■   *Chapter Four*   ■ ■ ■ ■ ■ ■

The Crisis of Faith and the
Promise of Grace

In mid-twentieth-century America the Divinity School of
the University of Chicago established a new field of study, that
of theology and literature. The departmental chairperson,
Nathan A. Scott Jr., led a vigorous academic inquiry in a series
of essays and books into what he liked to refer to as "the nature
of our period-style."[1] This curious phrase opened debate on
how to characterize the fiction of the 1940s, 1950s, and 1960s,
how that affected or connected to the prevailing atmosphere
of the Christianity of the times, particularly Protestant Christianity, and what Christian theology might have to benefit from
engaging in the conversation. Unlike the great modernist figures of the first half of the twentieth century, whose culture
provided a metaphysical, moral, and religious background,
the authors of his own time (1966), argues Scott, are insecure
and fundamentally alone because they do not have these cultural supports, neither to rest on nor to tilt against. Artists, he
thinks, need "systems of values" in which their art "could find

---

[1] Among Nathan A. Scott's many books, most significant are *Modern Literature and the Religious Frontier* (New York: Harper, 1958); *The Broken Center:
Studies in the Theological Horizon of Modern Literature* (New Haven, CT: Yale
University Press, 1966); and *Negative Capability: Studies in the New Literature
and the Religious Situation* (New Haven, CT: Yale University Press, 1969).

a principle of order and unity."[2] But instead we have "a literature of metaphysical isolation."[3] In his own times, says Scott,
the belief that God is silent, absent, or even dead is a product
of ignorance of "the gracious reality of presence."[4] What is
missing and needs to be restored is confidence in "the essential
healthiness of the things of the earth," and "the trauma that
has been suffered is the trauma inflicted upon the imagination
when it appears that both God and man are dead."[5]

The title of this present chapter pays homage to a particularly fruitful chapter in *The Broken Center*, where Scott sees
literature aiding the theology of his times to recover "a lively
awareness and certitude of Transcendence."[6] Admittedly, the
chapter does not name much of contemporary fiction, preferring instead to value Wordsworth's exploration of the powers
of the imagination. Deploring the "death of God" theologies
then prevalent in theological discussions, Scott quotes with
approval Jacques Maritain's observation that "poetry is ontology."[7] Scott believes that literature privileges the idea of
presence and "the sentiment of Being" that he thinks is missing
in the writings of such as Bishop John A. T. Robinson, Thomas
Altizer, and Paul van Buren.[8] In a later work Scott draws on
Goethe to show how art's attention to the particular can and
should lead beyond the thing itself. While looking understood
as sustained attention to the particular is vital to art, "mere
looking at a thing is of no use whatsoever," says Goethe. But

---

[2] Scott, *The Broken Center*, 7.

[3] Ibid., 8.

[4] Ibid., 18.

[5] Ibid., 19.

[6] Ibid., 177.

[7] Ibid., 178.

[8] For representative works of these three, see John A. T. Robinson, *Honest to God* (Philadelphia: Westminster, 1963); Thomas Altizer, *The Gospel of Christian Atheism* (Philadelphia: Westminster, 1966); and Paul van Buren, *The Secular Meaning of the Gospel* (New York: MacMillan, 1963).

looking "gradually merges into contemplation" and "contemplation into thinking." Because thinking is a matter of establishing connections, he continues, "it is possible to say that every attentive glance which we cast on the world is [ultimately] an act of theorizing."[9] The poetic vision attends to some concrete particular, but it suggests something more, "and thus its finite particularity affords a glass of vision into a kind of infinite depth and extension."[10] Paraphrasing Maritain, we might say that every act of authentic *poesis*, of making, implies a metaphysic. If we dwell long enough on the work of fiction, Henry James might say, we will eventually draw nearer to "the matter."

Today we do not live in the same situation in which Scott wrote half a century ago, but that does not mean his words are no longer valuable. Certainly, the death-of-God theologies of his time now seem faddish. That may be, however, because the logic of these theologies leads commonly to the abandonment of Christian traditions, while the reabsorption of theological voices into the conversation of Christian theology surely requires the death of death-of-God theologies. It is not easy to imagine liturgy or ritual inspired by a-theology, or a homily proclaiming the secular meaning of the gospel. So perhaps the voices that would have inherited the mantle of Robinson or Van Buren now speak on other matters from outside any connection to Christian theology. It is not a giant step from secular theology to secularity *tout court*. On the other side of the equation, today's literature does not on the whole display the kind of metaphysical or ontological concerns that Coleridge or Wordsworth did in their day, or that the great modernists of the early twentieth century like Joyce, Eliot, and Mann did in their time. Scott did not have much faith in the

[9] Quoted in Scott, *Negative Capability*, 22.
[10] Scott, *The Broken Center*, 181.

new fiction of his time, preferring to rest in the enduring values of classical literature. Much the same dissatisfaction is voiced today, particularly among those bemoaning the death or near-demise of the Catholic novel.[11] But the question needs to be rephrased in our times, when Catholic or indeed Christian culture can no longer be taken for granted.

One of Scott's shortcomings in the view of at least some critics is that he was too tied to an older modernist under-standing of both religion and literature and insufficiently aware of how postmodern literature had moved away from any sort of ethical or metaphysical concerns. Whether, indeed, Scott was guilty of this variety of blindness is by no means certain. What is clear is that to the degree that literature aban-dons interest in moral dilemmas, in the search for meaning and order, or in the role of the individual within some collec-tivity, in other words in community or communion, to that degree its usefulness as a stimulus to theological reflection is compromised. William Buhrman defends Scott from these criticisms, arguing that in his later work he moves beyond simplistic correlations between the truths of Christianity and the truths of fiction. Instead, as Scott illustrates in his book on Albert Camus,[12] literature substitutes the individual experience and search for meaning in a fundamentally open-ended and ambiguous reality. But somehow that search is there, even when there is no belief in a transcendent God as its anchor or locus.[13] Which in its turn may mean that although religious faith and literature have different origins and their own dis-crete authenticity, it is by no means clear that secular fiction has nothing to say to faith.

---

[11] This topic will be examined in chapter 6 below.

[12] Nathan A. Scott Jr., *Albert Camus* (New York: Hillary House, 1962).

[13] See William D. Buhrman, "Nathan Scott and Postmodern Testimony," *Christianity and Literature* 57, no. 3 (Spring 2008): 445–55.

Our Period-Style

One of the striking features of Nathan Scott's depiction of his times is the degree to which our own seems to mirror it. To Scott, his age was one of scientism, materialism, and the collapse of overarching systems of meaning that grounded social order. Neither religious nor philosophical values retained any objective weight or power. The consequence of this was that the whole responsibility for life was placed on the individual. As the Existentialist philosophers liked to say, life became a "project," the work of the individual. If this was interpreted, as it often was, as a triumph of human freedom, it also became clear that if negotiating one's own way through life perhaps offered a greater measure of authenticity than might seem to have accrued to a life of religious faith, it was going to be much more challenging and much less secure. Most people, of course, as Nietzsche had observed more than half a century earlier, just went on with their lives as if the death of God didn't change a thing. They became what Kierkegaard called "the public."[14] As Nietzsche put it, God was dead but the prophet who announced God's demise had come too soon. The public did not realize the extraordinarily radical implications of abandoning religious belief. No longer would there be any reason for a sense of order, a search for meaning, or a vision of ultimate purpose or destiny. Everything had changed, but it was going to take some time before the message sank in.

Today we might think that Nietzsche's moment has arrived, that the extent of secularism in today's world corresponds to Zarathustra's predictions, and yet it is not that simple. It is certainly true that traditional religious practice is in decline in the global north and that the ranks of the Nones are growing daily. Nevertheless, how do we take account of the growth of

---

[14] Soren Kierkegaard, *Two Ages* (Princeton, NJ: Princeton University Press, 2009), 26–36.

extremist violence in the name of religion and the substitution of materialist icons for belief in some transcendent reality, but at the same time link it to the prevailing insouciance of the postmodern pose, while also allowing for significant youthful altruism and an unfocused but real feeling of social insecurity and cultural precariousness? While Scott is right to make the claim that abandoning religion leads often to a lack of personal moorings, of a clear moral code or of any sense of community, replacing all of these with a more or less self-centered individualism, it is by no means clear that this is where the engine of history is inexorably moving. The truth is more complicated.

Since our discussion is one that relates religious belief and reading fiction, let us ask ourselves what these two seemingly disparate practices might have in common. More precisely, what might be the common explanation of their different *malaises*? Of course, they have much the same symptoms, namely, that both practices are becoming less and less popular. Serious reading and the practice of religion are not exactly dying out, but they seem to be becoming distinctly minority tastes. Stick your head inside most Christian churches any Sunday morning, or glance at the book display at your local Barnes and Noble, and you will immediately see the point. Looked at another way, they suffer from entirely different maladies. Historically speaking, religious faith has been the possession of ordinary folks more than their leaders, while serious reading was always an elite activity. And while the option of secularism can be a matter of principle and so, even when wrong, entirely authentic, the decision—if such it is—to stick with light fiction hardly fits into that category. Another similarity in the symptoms of their respective diseases is that what is substituted for either is in almost all cases something superficial. If someone stops going to church but takes up with a philosophical discussion group or engages in charitable activities, so be it. But to sleep in or watch youth soccer? And if someone gives up serious fiction in order to go find the time to learn to play a musical instrument or join a choir, who are we to object? But to fritter life away on social media? The end of reading and the end of church are not accidental, not at all.

It seems entirely probable that the similarities between the two kinds of illness might lead to one explanation for both and so perhaps to one course of action to cure them. One cannot, of course, say that abandoning formal religion or personal faith in God is exactly comparable to giving up reading substantial novels. But there is a striking association. Both display failure in the capacity for sustained attention. A crude way to say this is that staying in bed on Sunday morning or always choosing Dan Brown over Dostoevsky is the easy option, clearly a variety of mental laziness. The more sophisticated version of this argument is that there is a lapse of intentionality, using the term in the Sartrean sense more or less equivalent to consciousness.[15] Actions that are unthematized, that are unconscious or routine, do not display intentionality. Actions as the result of a more or less conscious decision are intentional. We know we do them and if challenged we could explain why we do or choose this rather than that.

To argue that a failure in sustained attention helps to explain both the decline in religious faith and in reading serious fiction is to signal the impoverishment of the human imagination. This affects most though not all individuals in the developed world, and it is exacerbated by social, cultural, and economic forces that unconsciously conspire to weaken this most human of all faculties. This is not to say that human beings no longer display a high degree of creativity. Probably it is just as much in evidence as ever, but it may well be that creativity has been siphoned off into certain activities and is no longer available for others. Thank God that we have immense creativity in

---

[15] See Jean-Paul Sartre, "Intentionality: A Fundamental Idea of Husserl's Phenomenology," *Journal of the British Society for Phenomenology* 1, no. 2 (1970): 4–5.

science and technology, though the ability to decide how to make that creativity work for good and not evil is not of itself a skill of the creative person. It requires a different kind of imagination, namely, moral imagination, which a person may or may not possess. But do we really need the extent of creativity displayed in today's marketing media? Even such a banal thing as a TV commercial is often highly creative but bereft of moral imagination. And if you respond with, "Of course, commercials are imaginative!" then recall the Coleridgean distinction. What looks like imagination may be and probably is its lesser sister, mere fancy.

The power of the moral or Coleridgean sense of imagination is that which enables us to go from attention to the particular in all its concreteness to some kind of apprehension of the whole which gives it its meaning. This is what the medieval theologians were talking about when they distinguished faith from natural religion. Of course, it is possible to have a kind of notional understanding of what faith might be by the use of reason, but making the act of faith required a nonrational but not irrational embrace of the object of faith. As a consequence of this act of faith in the ineffable, of this act of love of the mysterious power whose being the believer can never totally grasp this side of the grave, life was dramatically changed. Conversion means that nothing is the same any longer, because everything now has its place in the great scheme of things that is the gift of grace.

The problem of faith today and the problem of writing/reading today are so closely related because the problem lies not in the faith or in the literature so much as in the human subject. In a word, the problem is individualism. It is this that characterizes what Scott calls "our period style," but today the term may not be sufficiently strong. It is not so much a style as it is the temper of our times as a product of many different cultural and especially political currents. The accusation leveled against Scott that he was antiquated in his understanding and unable to come to terms with the different situation of the early postmodernism of the 1960s is misplaced. If his analysis has a weakness it is that he did not see "period-style" as something that oppressed or curtailed human freedom, perhaps because recent history had provided examples of much more brutal forms of repression that made the subtleties of something more insidious less likely to come to public recognition.

Toward a Theology of the Imagination

If today we know that an excessive focus on the individual, on individual freedoms, and on attainment mark our times (our period-style), it is also true that communities of faith and the arts in general, especially literature, have the capacity to counter radical individualism. At their best, both insist on sustained attention to the particular as a path to the recognition that there is something larger than ourselves to which we need to attend if life is to have the richness that is its *telos*. Religious faith is intensely communal and of its nature places the individual in contact with God or some sense of the transcendent that, while it values the individual, sees his or her destiny bound up with something much larger than the self. Literature at the very least invites encounter with beauty, tragedy, or comedy in a way that places the individual in a similarly larger context in which his or her sense of self can be enriched or enlarged. Both in their different ways offer a gift, either or both of which it would be wise to accept if we do not wish to be fundamentally isolated in our own egoism, or in some *égoisme à deux*.

It is unfortunately also true that religion is not always at its best and indeed that it too can be infected by the temper of our times so that it becomes a more or less unwitting ally of culture's overemphasis on the individual. Only something like this can explain how a Catholic tradition that has at its center the idea of the communion of saints—that the whole community of

believers living and dead belongs and works and prays together—can, at least in the United States, see its Catholic faithful deeply implicated in the individualism of popular culture
instead of standing against it in countercultural solidarity with
the whole human family. The church—which for most people
means the pulpit—is to blame for promoting the idea of salvation as an individual project or at best a gift to the individual
for his or her personal fidelity. Prominent Catholic public figures can nod in the direction of Ayn Rand while everyday
Catholics can sign on to political initiatives that exacerbate
income inequality, even if it is not to their own benefit.

It is also unfortunately true that literature can be seduced
by "our period-style" into an intense focus on the individual
or the particular that the writer is unable or unwilling to move
beyond to the larger frame of reference in which questions of
meaning can arise. To say that much contemporary fiction
suffers from this limitation is in no way to judge the literary
skill that these works often demonstrate. David Foster Wallace
addressed this issue at length in an interview conducted by
Larry McCaffery.[16] Wallace sees TV and popular films and what
he calls "most kinds of 'low art,'" which really exist just to
make money, recognizing "that audiences prefer 100 percent
pleasure to the reality that tends to be 49 percent pleasure and
51 percent pain." "Serious" art, on the other hand, which is
not primarily about making money, "is more apt to make you
uncomfortable, or to force you to work hard to access its pleasures, the same way that in real life true pleasure is usually a
by-product of hard work and discomfort." The trouble, then,
is that the public, especially the younger public, expect art to
be 100 percent pleasurable, and effortlessly so. They are not
stupid, but they are trained "to be sort of lazy and childish"

---

[16] "An Interview with David Foster Wallace," *Review of Contemporary Fiction*
13, no. 2 (Summer 1993): 127–50.

in their expectations. The consequence is that art that requires effort is a hard sell.

The mental conditioning that makes what is hard to do less attractive also has its parallel among writers themselves, who may respond to this particular social ill by abdicating their responsibilities as creative artists. The easy path to take, thinks Wallace, is to mirror the malaise of the times by "slapping together stories with characters who are stupid, vapid, emotionally retarded, which is easy, because these sorts of characters require no development." So, "bad writing becomes an ingenious mimesis of a bad world." In what are obviously dark times, he muses, "do we need fiction that does nothing but dramatize how dark and stupid everything is?" Surely "the definition of good art would seem to be art that locates and applies CPR to those elements of what's human and magical that still live and glow despite the times' darkness." And he concludes that "really good fiction could have as dark a world-view as it wished, but it'd find a way both to depict this world and to illuminate the possibilities for being alive and human in it."

Wallace has put his finger on the characteristic that enables us to distinguish serious fiction from that which is apparently serious but is in fact less so, and indeed that may be less authentic than some of the "lower" forms that exist simply to entertain. Wallace himself admits to watching enormous amounts of TV, and most of it has to be what we would call "escapist." There is nothing wrong with this, any more than there is a problem with reading thrillers or detective fiction or even romance novels, so long as the reader can resist the conditioning that tells her or him that *this* is what art is, merely a pleasurable exercise. Wallace demonstrates in his creative writing what he discusses at length in this essay, namely, that pain and suffering pay a large part in human life and that art must pay attention, but not give it the last word. So, he says, "I strongly suspect a big part of real art fiction's job is to aggravate this sense of entrapment and loneliness and death in people, to move people to countenance it, since any possible human redemption requires us first to face what's dreadful, what we want to deny." In other words, art must address the pain and suffering in life but not simply mirror it. It is striking to see Wallace imply that "redemption" is where serious fiction is heading.

It would be wrong to conclude from Wallace's analysis that serious fiction can be taken up only with pain and suffering, any more than we should think that pain and suffering are the only serious human experiences. Wallace's point is surely that the background awareness of all human lives is their finitude, that we know we will die. Whatever pain and suffering there is in any one life—and which life has none of either?—brings the person face-to-face with the limit-questions of ultimacy and meaning. The mistake of much contemporary fiction is that it doesn't raise those questions or even allow them but simply describes, often very skillfully, the character, the experience, or the situation in such a way that it does not open a door beyond itself. Speaking in purely secular terms for a moment, Wallace is presumably thinking that while the depiction of the dark side of life is something that serious fiction must address, it also needs to push through to joy. Joy, unlike mere pleasure, can coexist with pain and suffering and most certainly with grief. We may grieve at the death of a loved one, but the life they have led is a source of joy. We will have much more to say about the relationship between pleasure and joy or happiness in the final chapter of the book.

Nathan Scott's reflections in *The Broken Center* on the genres of tragedy and comedy expand on and enrich this picture.[17] In some respects they correct Wallace's analysis, and in others they reinforce it. So, for example, Scott is clear that tragedy is

[17] "The Tragic Vision and the Christian Faith," 119–44, and "The Bias of Comedy and the Narrow Escape into Faith," 77–118.

not fundamentally about pain and suffering, and equally sure that comedy is a serious matter. And, while there is pleasure in both literary genres, both point beyond themselves to something more profound and, perhaps, ultimately ineffable.

Scott's discussion of comedy comes in the context of considering the work of Camus, who is certainly not normally considered as a comic writer.[18] Discussing the "cosmic homelessness" that he associates with our "period-style," Scott identifies Camus as a proponent of "a quieter kind of humanism." In Camus's atheistic vision, Scott identifies an effort "to redeem the time by sacramentalizing the relation between man and man."[19] To explain this he turns to the figure of Charlie Chaplin in his classic silent movies, the utterly human little figure who is "a kind of icon of the human actuality." In Chaplin we see our own frailty, and the comic man makes us accept our contingency and our humanity. Invoking also the figure of Falstaff rejected by Shakespeare's Henry, he suggests that our sympathy for him provokes "the comic catharsis which restores our confidence in the realm of finitude." True, there are some comic figures at whom we just laugh, but the richer kind is the one like Chaplin or Falstaff, where our laughter is accompanied by sympathy. Indeed, for all his faults, Falstaff "*is* a man, always and intensely human—and this, I take it, is why he is the great saint of Western comedy." He is not only a saint but also a hero, "the archetypal instance of the comic *hero*," because "he is so deeply rooted in the human condition that he restores our confidence in its resilience."[20]

In our discussion thus far we have frequently noted the importance of the concretely particular leading us somehow beyond itself to a deeper reality or "matter" that we cannot

---

[18] Classically, of course, a comedy is not identified so much for being humorous as for the harmonious resolution with which it ends.

[19] Scott, *The Broken Center*, 78.

[20] Ibid., 107–8.

fully grasp, and this indeed is the meaning of sacramentality. The concrete that points beyond itself to the mysterious, that gives us an always partial but nevertheless real glimpse of mystery, is sacramental. So, Chaplin and Falstaff and others like them—perhaps *Twelfth Night*'s Malvolio would be a further example—are sacramental figures. But in the profoundly incarnational Christian dispensation they also remind us of the value of the concrete in itself. So, they are sacraments of a mystery that surrounds us, embodied in the earth we call our home. They bring us back to the holiness of our finitude. As Christopher Fry wrote, "Comedy is an escape, not from truth but from despair: a narrow escape into faith."[21]

Turning to tragedy, Scott quotes Jaspers's opinion that it occurs "wherever the powers that collide are true independently of one another."[22] There is always a moral dilemma in tragedy, two competing goods of which only one can be chosen, or two competing evils of which one must be chosen. The *hubris* of the tragic hero, so often interpreted as simple pride, is actually the recognition that in the face of the tragic dilemma it is necessary to accept one's own destiny to choose. So the tragic hero becomes the guilty one, committed to partiality, revealing finitude and contingency. The tragic hero is both weak and strong: the former because the choice is always imperfect; the latter because the courage to choose what is imperfect is its own kind of moral quality. Even when they are most wrong, as Lear and Othello surely are, there is something with which to identify, even to admire. Duped as they both are, they choose. They choose the wrong thing, but they choose.

Why is it that religion and literature have headed off down the wrong path? In a 1961 essay Iris Murdoch offered a very

---

[21] Christopher Fry, "Comedy," *Tulane Drama Review* 4 (March 1960): 77, quoted in Scott, *The Broken Center*, 117.

[22] Scott, *The Broken Center*, 124.

similar response to that of Scott and Wallace.[23] In our scientific and antimetaphysical age, she writes, "the dogmas, images, and precepts of religion have lost much of their power," while the philosophical influences of liberalism in the West and Marxism in the East have undermined any deep understanding of human personality. Literature could respond to this situation, but the temptation of all but the greatest art "is to console." Modern writers attempt to console us by myths or stories, in which truth is "sincerity" and imagination is "fantasy." But what we need is something more substantial, "to be enabled to think in terms of degrees of freedom" and "to picture, in a non-metaphysical, non-totalitarian and non-religious sense, the transcendence of reality." And literature can achieve such an end, thinks Murdoch, holding up Camus as an example, if it makes the attempt to speak the truth. Not simply sincerity, but truth. Challenging one of the most influential critical approaches of her time, she argues that form itself can be a temptation because it can make the work of art "into a small myth which is a self-contained and indeed self-satisfied individual." The remedy for the consolations of form is a focus on character, where we meet the contingency that mirrors the incompleteness of reality: "Real people are destructive of myth, contingency is destructive of fantasy and opens the way for imagination."

Constructing a theology of the imagination requires religion to take account of the therapeutic value of literature. It is good literature that helps refine our sensibilities and returns us to a proper sense of the role of the imagination. Contrariwise, literature can find in religion and in the Christian story in particular a rich mine of imaginative symbols that point beyond themselves to a vision of the whole. But the Christian scholar embarking on a theology of the imagination is doing so in the same real, secular world that the agnostic or atheistic writer

---

[23] Iris Murdoch, "Against Dryness," *Encounter* (January 1961): 16–20.

inhabits. There is no special Christian world and no particular Christian vision of reality that can exist independently of the wisdom and the suffering of the everyday world. There are truly Christian insights, but they cannot be vigorously maintained in isolation from the wisdom of the world. Christians have no exclusive purchase on truth, and the central figure of Jesus Christ in the Christian story is of someone who is simultaneously living in the everyday world and—in the faith of Christian believers—revealing something essential and absolutely true about the fundamentally inaccessible mystery of God. It is Jesus of Nazareth in the world who is the face of the absolute other, but any easy certitude is undermined by the painful realities of his suffering and death. And if Christians believe that in the figure of Jesus Christ they glimpse something of that meaning of the whole that is ultimately true, they are also intimately related to and in a way dependent on the dwelling on the pain and suffering of everyday life that is so often the context of the greatest literature. If the reality of evil in the world cannot finally overcome belief, since Christ himself undergoes and triumphs over suffering, belief in its turn cannot deny the obscenity of evil, since the evil of pain, suffering, and violent death is integral to the presence of God in history in Jesus Christ.

"*To Be a Man*": The Plague

Albert Camus's novel, *La Peste* (*The Plague*), was first published in 1947 and appeared in English a year later.[24] The book tells the story of an outbreak of bubonic plague in the Algerian coastal town of Oran, which requires its isolation from all outsiders and places a ban on traveling out of the town lest the plague be spread more widely. The central character is a local

---

[24] Albert Camus, *The Plague*, trans. Stuart Gilbert (New York: Random House, 1991).

physician, Dr. Bernard Rieux, and the story is told by a narrator who remains anonymous for most of the account, supplemented by extensive extracts from the journals of Jean Tarrou. Among the other important characters are the Jesuit priest Fr. Paneloux; a curious self-proclaimed writer, Joseph Grand; the black marketeer Cottard; Raymond Rambert (a journalist from elsewhere trapped in the city when the plague erupts); and Monsieur Othon, a magistrate. There are only two women of any significance in the story, Rieux's saintly mother and his wife, who at the beginning of the story goes off to a sanatorium in another city to be treated for tuberculosis. The other major character, in some ways the most important of all, is the collective population of Oran, from their unthinking materialism at the beginning, through the trials of the time of the plague, to their equally mindless euphoria when the plague is finally over. They are a perfect example of Kierkegaard's "public" and they share many characteristics of the shallow populace about whom Wallace and Murdoch have had much to say.

The Plague explores the question of what it is to be a human being by examining human behavior in a time of great stress. It does not matter if we read the novel as a straightforward account of a city under siege from a dreaded disease or if we see it as a parable of French life under Nazi occupation. In both cases—and both have their proponents and their justice—the challenge is the same. When we have no belief in anything transcendent, in anything beyond this life, what guides our conduct when everything that is happening is yelling at us to take cover and take care of our own lives? A religious person ought to find it relatively easy to give up self-concern for the good of others, though often enough this is not what happens to believers under stress. And an atheist ought to have no particular grounds for caring for the collective, though frequently this is the case. So, why would an individual who thought there was nothing beyond this life and had no theoretical justification for caring for those he or she did not love enter into a life of altruism? And what would this tell us about what exactly it is to be a human being? This is where Camus takes us.

Rieux is the still center of *The Plague*. The dreaded fever moves in waves, the plague is never still, and the men who surround Rieux in the story all move and change in different ways. Cottard enters the story as a failed suicide and moves on to a successful career as a black marketeer. Grand seems at first a foolish little man trapped in a ridiculous quest to write. Rambert wants to escape the town and tries hard. Othon is a pompous ass who eventually loses his young son to the plague and is quarantined himself. Tarrou begins as a journal keeper who wants to be a saint but doesn't believe in God. But all of them become something more in the time that Oran is overwhelmed by the plague. Even Fr. Paneloux the scholar manages to enlarge his sensibilities, as we get to see by comparing his two sermons.

Although every one of these characters has his own backstory, each of them develops in the direction of caring for something beyond themselves or those to whom they are closest. Their starting point is where the populace of Oran as a whole begins, business-oriented, dull, complacent, and—though Camus does not use this word—unreflective. Rieux himself is not the typical resident of the city. He is "a man who was sick and tired of the world he lived in" but "had much liking for his fellow men" and "had resolved . . . to have no truck with injustice and compromises with the truth" (21). He is, in fact, very like Camus as his contemporaries knew him, even those like Jean-Paul Sartre who were quite ambivalent about their very on-and-off friendship. He is a deeply thoughtful person, as indeed is Tarrou, who only wants "peace of mind" but also seeks ways to avoid wasting time "by being fully aware of it all the time" (26). Unlike Rieux he was immediately attracted by the ugliness of the town and fascinated by its business orientation. Tarrou's journal and the unnamed author of the narrative, unsurprisingly revealed late in the book to be Rieux himself, together make up the text. The other characters are always reported on.

What, then, is going on with the transformation of these minor characters? It seems that there is something about living through the horrifying experience of the plague that brings out of them a kind of altruism. They all, eventually, volunteer to work with the victims in one way or another, a course of action that inevitably makes it more rather than less likely that they will contract the disease. The weakest human being of them all appears initially to be Joseph Grand, described as having "all the attributes of insignificance" and *permanently* occupying the post of *"temporary* assistant municipal clerk" (44). He eventually reveals he is writing a book, though his case of writer's block is about as severe as one can imagine. And yet Rieux finds his life exemplary, being "one of those rare people . . . who have the courage of their good feelings" (46). Rambert the journalist spends most of the story attempting to escape the town, but he eventually volunteers to help Rieux while he awaits his opportunity and finally abandons the attempt to leave. The magistrate Othon is transformed by the loss of his son into someone ready and willing, after his release from quarantine, to return to the camp to help those still being held. Tarrou, unlike the other minor characters, has interacted closely with Rieux from the beginning. All of these choices, including those of Rieux himself, have a lot to do with love, whether present, lost, or unrequited. Grand's regret that his own failures led to the end of his marriage, Rambert's pining for his girlfriend, Rieux's concern for his sick wife, Tarrou's past, and Othon's surprising depth of love for his son, all somehow work to loosen the self-absorption to which anyone in the plague-stricken city could succumb.

The two sermons that Fr. Paneloux preaches during the plague provide a good example of the workings of what a religious person would call grace. In the first, horrifying sermon, where the plague is God's judgment and wake-up call, Paneloux deals out fear and guilt upon the packed church but ends surprisingly with the hope that *all* in Oran "would offer up to heaven that one prayer which is truly Christian, a prayer of love" (99). By the time of his second sermon he is a changed man, no longer the distant scholar but now deeply involved with Rieux in working with the sick and dying. This time the preacher uses the language of "we" rather than the "you" of the first preaching, but the message is, if anything, harder. In time of plague, says Paneloux, God requires "the greatest of all virtue: that of the All or Nothing" (225). In a Dostoevskian moment Paneloux refuses to try to explain away the suffering of a child. While he does not follow the path of Ivan Karamazov's refusal to believe in the face of the suffering of the innocent, he poses the same challenge: "My brothers, a time of testing has come for us all. We must believe everything or deny everything. And who among you, I ask, would dare to deny everything?" (224).

Rieux clearly cannot go along with Paneloux's conviction that "all trials, however cruel, worked together for good to the Christian" (223). At the end of the very graphic account of the suffering and death of M. Othon's young son, Rieux fiercely declares his innocence, to which Paneloux responds that what they had just witnessed was as unbearable to him as to the atheist doctor. Paneloux sympathizes with Rieux's anger, recognizing that his revulsion is because we cannot understand what happened. "But," he adds, "perhaps we should love what we cannot understand." No, says Rieux, "until my dying day I shall refuse to love a scheme of things in which children are put to torture" (218). Paneloux responds sadly (and frankly, enigmatically), "I've just realized what is meant by 'grace.'" And when Rieux admits this is something he does not possess but that the important thing for the moment is that the two of them are working side by side to the same end, the relief of suffering, Paneloux concludes, "Yes, yes . . . you, too, are working for man's salvation" (219).

The most revealing of the conversations in *The Plague* are the two that take place between Rieux and Tarrou, the first at the doctor's house and the second sitting one evening on the rooftops of Oran. The occasion of the first is Tarrou's visit to explain his plan for teams of voluntary helpers to aid in combatting the plague and his welcome promise to participate himself. When Rieux tries to get Tarrou to acknowledge that he is aware of the consequences of doing this voluntary work, he responds with a question: "Do you believe in God, Doctor?" Rieux equivocates a little, though his response is mostly negative, and then he adds that "since the world is shaped by death, mightn't it be better for God if we refuse to believe in Him and struggle with all our might against death, without raising our eyes toward the heaven where He sits in silence?" (128). And when he pushes Tarrou to explain why he decided to help, Tarrou invokes his "code of morals." "What code?" asks Rieux, and receives the one word answer, "Comprehension" (130). The second conversation begins with Tarrou's long account of how he came to be unalterably opposed to the death penalty and what this cost him. But when we see, he thinks, that we are all implicated in the culture of death that it implies, then "each of us has the plague within him" and "no one on earth is free from it." Nevertheless, we all have to work to eradicate this plague within us, to side with the victims and not the pestilences, in the hope of joining one day the tiny group of "true healers," achieved along "the path of sympathy." Tarrou admits that what interests him "is learning how to become a saint," but "can one be a saint without God?" Rieux simply says that he feels more fellowship with the victims than with the saints. "What interests me," he adds, "is being a man." To which Tarrou responds, "Yes, we're both after the same thing, but I'm less ambitious" (255). And then, in what can only be described as a sacramental moment, they cement their friendship by going swimming in the ocean together. "Neither had said a word, but they were conscious of being perfectly at one, and the memory of this night would be cherished by them both" (257).

Beyond the echoes of Dostoevsky and something of the flavor of Graham Greene (Rieux could have been taken from the pages of any Greene novel), there is a lot here that would have furnished an exciting conversation between Camus and Bonhoeffer. Perhaps Bonhoeffer could not have gone all the way with Rieux's suggestion that refusing to believe in God and struggling instead against human suffering is the way to behave, though the sentiment seems very close to Bonhoeffer's statement that "it is not the religious act that makes the Christian, but participation in the sufferings of God in the secular life."[25] And he would have a lot of sympathy with the rejection of the kind of God Rieux is imagining, one who "sits in silence" in heaven. Similarly, Rieux's remark to Tarrou that no one in the world, not even Paneloux, believed in an all-powerful God, though Paneloux certainly "believed that he believed in such a God," would have interested the Lutheran pastor. No one, said Rieux, "ever threw himself on Providence completely" (127). For both Rieux and Bonhoeffer, it would seem, we ought to live "as if God did not exist." And for both, the important thing is not religion, still less doctrine, but human suffering. This way lies salvation, and it is this that led Paneloux to see his basic brotherhood with Rieux.

Fiction helps to complicate what religion would like to represent as a simple matter. So, one of the great challenges to religious belief today, particularly but not only in Christianity, is the tension between believing in one's own tradition and yet leaving room for the mercy of God to be at work among all human beings. The more we incline toward the latter, in fact toward some kind of belief in universal salvation, the harder it is to justify the superiority of one's own sacred story.

---

[25] Dietrich Bonhoeffer, *Letters and Papers from Prison: The Enlarged Edition*, ed. Eberhard Bethge (London: The Folio Society, 2000), 323.

And the less willing we are to consider it superior, the less significant it seems to be to adhere to it rather than to some other or to no one story in particular. Thus, the flight of the Nones. In the not-so-distant past, Catholics and Protestants alike were all too ready to proclaim the primacy of a Christian understanding of history and a belief that Jesus Christ is the universal savior, wielded as if this were a battle-axe with which to mow down the hordes of heathens if not, indeed, also those Christians on the other side of the Catholic/Protestant divide. Today, relatively few people hold to this narrow understanding of salvation, and there are many who simply want to sideline it in favor of an essentially sentimental understanding of universal salvation. But neither extreme, nor the majority somewhere in the middle, find it easy to justify the nuanced picture that needs to emerge by reference to the theological convictions of their own perspective on the Christian tradition. This is an important moment in which fiction steps in to aid the religious imagination.

The strength of fiction's value to the religious imagination depends not only on its reluctance to eschew ambiguity but also on its steady focus on the complexity of the human person. So, it not only issues a warning call to the inclination of religion to present complex issues as simpler than they are. It also reminds religion what it so often forgets, that it has far more to say about the nature of human life than it does about the character of divine life. God we do not know as we know everything else that we know, and if the Christian genius has been to break through the ignorance by faith in a human being as the revelation of God in history, it is *as a human being* that Jesus Christ is held to reveal the nature of divinity. The doctrine of incarnation makes *human* history revelatory of God, as Nathan Scott argued so forcefully, so what happens in the messy course of human history or in the complexities of an individual human life is grist to the mill of the religious imagination. The human story and human stories reveal the holy, whether or not we wish to name it God, and the most gifted storytellers bring their readers into contact with what Matisse called "the deep gravity that persists in every human being."[26] Fiction is so particular to time and place, so focused on an individual or a group of them, and yet—if it is of sufficient quality—constantly pressing toward the whole, to the "matter" that lies somehow beyond it. Religion, and so at times the imagination of believers, is often inclined to think that it can go straight to the matter. When it fails, or falters, in this impossible task, fiction is there to receive the believer back into the real work of the imagination, where ambiguity and complexity and indirectness hold sway.

Moral fiction like all of Camus's work, but especially *The Plague*, insists with force on the religious imagination's capacity for revisioning. In *The Plague* we are enveloped in the bathetic normalcy of the crowd, of the unreflective masses who inhabit Oran. For the most part they endure the pestilence with a certain measure of fatalism, only as it finally ends to descend back into what Camus calls "tawdry exuberance," a condition that suggests they have learned nothing at all from the experience. Without paying particular attention, Camus also makes clear that the city's religious culture is predominantly Catholic, at least insofar as religion has much impact at all. The church is full for Paneloux's first sermon, somewhat less so for the second. But for the most part religious faith plays little apparent role in the lives of Oran's citizens and almost none at all in the real focus of the book, on Rieux and the little band of men around him. Nevertheless, the novel as a whole raises the fundamental but not exclusively religious question, "what is a human being?"

Because the background to *The Plague* is an account of terrible suffering and death on a large scale, any Christian

---

[26] Henri Matisse, "Notes of a Painter," in *Matisse on Art*, ed. Jack Flam (Oakland: University of California Press, 1995), 43.

response has to be couched in terms of theodicy. Paneloux's two sermons show how this might work. The first sees the suffering as just punishment for sin, while the second calls for blind faith. Neither of these solutions is entirely satisfactory, like any other effort to produce a cogent explanation for why God is not to blame for evil. But the second is more sophisticated, explained perhaps by Paneloux's growth in moral stature. He does not say that the appropriate response to suffering and evil is blind faith but rather that in the face of suffering and evil the believer must recognize that there can be no gaps in the fabric of faith. You either accept the whole thing, or you reject the whole thing. You cannot believe in God with any kind of authenticity and not accept that there is such a thing as innocent suffering. Even if the option for faith is affirmed and the ultimate cannot be revealed to be tragic, nevertheless there is tragedy within the fundamentally comic narrative. The cross is tragedy, and the Christian conviction that it ultimately gives way to new life must be held in a form of hope that does not simply cancel out the tragic.

The value to the religious imagination of work like that of Camus is, then, that it demands that people of faith hold to their faith in full awareness of the challenge that secular reality and its attendant human suffering represent. Exactly as Fr. Paneloux's second sermon insists, the Christian must accept all or nothing, must will the death of the innocent because God wills it, "must choose either to hate God or to love God" (228). Camus himself, we can be sure, thought that this kind of belief is impossible or at least irrational. Like Ivan Karamazov, he rejected the God who could cause innocent suffering and, like Nietzsche, he maintained the need for a high moral posture. Yes, life is absurd, but human authenticity consists in living "as if it were not." In *The Plague*, most of the principal characters are agnostic or atheist. But collectively they illustrate a form of life in the face of human suffering that is exactly that which people of faith need also to adopt. The difference between Paneloux and Rieux, we hear, is that the priest knows "grace" that the doctor does not possess or recognize.

It also may be the case that *The Plague* forces the person of faith to confront the question of who this God can be who is so sufficiently innocent of causing suffering that the suffering does not lead to the rejection of God. The all or nothing that Paneloux demands of the one confronting faith and suffering is accurate if it means that a believer must accept the inevitability of human suffering and the nonexistence of the God who would step in on every or even any occasion to mitigate or remove the suffering. It would not be acceptable if it meant that the person of faith must accept the "all" of innocent suffering in a world in which God could and should protect us from innocent suffering. But as Camus pointed out, even Paneloux cannot believe in a perfect Providence. The facts of human existence simply do not allow such a conclusion and efforts to "make sense" of a child's suffering are simply obscene. Rieux makes no effort to make sense of any of it because his certitude lay in "the daily round. . . . The thing was to do your job as it should be done" (41).

If the religious believer is able to accept the "all" and somehow continue to believe in a God who must be reimagined in order not to be guilty of innocent suffering, then the question arises to what degree the faith of such a believer actually differs from the absence of faith in a Rieux or a Tarrou. Both types of people work to alleviate the suffering of the plague victims. The atheist does so in the conviction that there is no higher power that could intervene to help, while the believer collaborates in the same efforts in the conviction that God will not or does not intervene and that human efforts at succor are all that are available. If it is true that the only eyes that God has are our eyes, the only hands that God has are our hands, then at the height of the plague, it is no surprise that the eyes and hands of believers are exactly as strong or as weak as those of atheists. The atheist knows that there is no God to come to our aid, and the believer knows that we must act "as if God did not exist."

If this is the stand-off that *The Plague* leaves us with, it is nevertheless true that the sheer brilliance of Camus's narrative forces believers to take issue with its conclusions. Not that Camus is necessarily wrong, but maybe that Paneloux is wrong in a way that Camus could not have seen or have wanted to represent. It is quite noticeable that in neither of Paneloux's sermons does Jesus Christ get a look in or is the mystery of incarnation referred to at all. While Paneloux grows in human sensitivity between the two sermons, most probably because of his decision to assist in Rieux's work, his God remains a fairly remote and somewhat relentless figure. As R. W. B. Lewis puts it, Camus's quarrel with God was "marked by some pretty inaccurate firing."[27] With direct reference to *The Myth of Sisyphus*, Lewis commented drily that "the God whom Camus, following Nietzsche, had declared dead was a God who in fact had not been alive very long; he had been created in the polemics of Martin Luther."[28] Paneloux cannot be expected to display more theological capaciousness than his creator, and it shows in his odd reference to grace. Grace, he thinks, is what distinguishes him from Rieux. It is grace that enables Paneloux to love what he cannot understand, even the God who wills the death of the innocent, while it is the absence of grace that leads Rieux to say in response that his idea of love is very different, that as long as he lives he "will refuse to love a scheme of things in which children are put to the torture" (218). What fails Paneloux is the insight that in a religion of incarnation God is fully present in a suffering and dying human being, and that this signals the weakness of God in face of the human condition. This is not an easy thought and is not surprisingly

[27] R. W. B. Lewis, *The Picaresque Saint: A Critical Study* (New York: Lippincott, 1956), 78.
[28] Ibid., 59.

beyond Camus's theological insight, but it is a deepening of the religious imagination for which *The Plague* can be accounted responsible for anyone lucky enough to read it.

Rieux feels challenged "to be a man." Bonhoeffer declares that "to be a Christian does not mean to be religious in a particular way . . . but to be a man."[29] These two convictions are not identical but they are surely related. The difference is rooted in Bonhoeffer's faith in Christ; the similarity lies in their focus on the task of being human in this world on this day in this place. Bonhoeffer is moved by the need to conform one's life to that of Christ, the Christ who was human and who suffered and died, who established a pattern of life, following which can be called "discipleship." Rieux is moved by a thirst for justice, a distaste for injustice, and compassion for those who suffer. The victims, not the saints, are those with whom he chooses to identify. When Paneloux and Rieux recognize that they must work together to defeat the plague, they are not so much calling a truce as they are affirming what must always be the priority of the needs of concrete humanity over the words we use to express why self-giving is essential. And as Bonhoeffer asserted, the Gospel exists *for this life*. God wants us to get on with things *etsi deus non daretur*, and Jesus Christ is to be our model of freedom. As William Lynch puts it, "Autonomy is not a defiance, but a grace."[30]

---

[29] Bonhoeffer, *Letters and Papers*, 323.

[30] William Lynch, *Christ and Prometheus: A New Image of the Secular* (Notre Dame, IN: University of Notre Dame Press, 1970), 140.

Chapter Five

Secular Mysticism

Is the Novel about More Than Itself?

Thus far we have privileged those fictions that seem to point beyond themselves to a "matter" which they may not grasp or even know about but which teases author and reader alike toward a taste of transcendence. We have, in fact, tended to identify novels that have this component as serious or substantial fiction, consigning those others—where there is nothing beyond itself—to the category of light reading. Iser started us down this path with his distinction between work to which we take an attitude and that which invites interpretation. The example of the difference between a Margery Allingham mystery and a work of Dostoevsky was an effort to point clearly to the difference. The detective fiction may be extraordinarily well written, could in some examples be much better written than many a "serious" work of fiction, but is nevertheless in most if not all cases simply about itself. When queried about the book, we would simply tell the story and feel that we had done it justice, hopefully without revealing the identity of the murderer. "Serious" fiction introduces into the space between the reader and the text the something more that the author intends to hint at, and even the "matter" that is not entirely clear to the author, so that in the act of reading the reader creates what Iser calls "the aesthetic object." In telling someone about this kind of reading we would certainly offer some kind of interpretation that went beyond the surface meaning of the text. To use the well-worn phrase, there is a surplus of meaning that neither we nor any other reader will ever exhaust.

There are two separable but related ways in which this neat and, to some, over-convenient distinction can be challenged. One challenge comes from literary theorists; the other from novelists themselves. The first of the two is occasioned by those critics, beginning in the mid-twentieth century, whom we may broadly call postmodern theorists. These critics are unimpressed by conventionally realistic fictions, some of them arguing that all these books do is smuggle some ideology or other into the text and so into the consciousness of the reader, while others—moved in many cases by semiotics and inheriting the critical approach of the influential New Criticism created earlier in the century—insist on viewing fictions as internally self-referential sets of signs and symbols. The first group would argue that the realistic novel is not realistic at all, and the second that it is not about anything beyond itself. Authorial intention, still more so biography, is irrelevant. The other challenge is that which is issued by novelists who seem to have no interest in anything beyond the descriptive process they employ, who wish perhaps to delineate shades of consciousness but who reject any attempt to discover meaning beyond the process of consciousness itself. Who may claim, in other words, that their work is serious but, in the end, only about itself.

Mark Edmundson addresses the dangers of literary theory. He writes in *Why Read?* of the debilitating effect of introducing undergraduate students to the work of thinkers like Foucault or Derrida. The problem is not that their ideas are unworthy of attention but rather that their ideas are often adopted uncritically—by teachers as often as by students—and applied to literary works in a reductive manner. So, says Edmundson, if Foucault is used uncritically to look at the work of Dickens, "you lose what benefit Foucault may bring," and if you translate Dickens into Foucault, "you lose what benefit Dickens might have had to deliver."[1] James Wood tackles the problem of theory in a similar way in his discussion of Roland Barthes's critique of realism. According to Wood, Barthes's view that conventional fictions are "merely a set of conventions and codes" leads him to conclude that realistic fiction isn't about reality but about realism. And realism isn't true. Wood comments that "fiction is of course a form of lying." But just because realistic fiction is not itself reality, this does not mean that "conventional realism can never disclose the real."[2]

The challenge mounted by novelists who want to argue with Barthes that their work is a set of conventions and codes with no connection to the real is addressed in a series of blistering essays written fifty years ago by Nathan Scott Jr. Scott excoriates what he calls "the new *alittérature*," which he identifies above all with the work of Alain Robbe-Grillet and Roland Barthes. In the view of Robbe-Grillet and others, writes Scott, narrative literature needs to dispense with plot, character, and eloquence, since these aspects of the literary tradition actually falsify "the existential reality." Writers will catalog things, for, in Robbe-Grillet's words, "the world is neither significant nor absurd. It [simply] is." So, comments Scott, this produces "a fiction from which the human presence has been most rigorously expunged, in which the single subject matter is formed by the novelist's descriptions of the angles, planes, and surfaces of the world."[3] The novel is what it is. There is no intention and no justification for looking at it as trying, however subtly or implicitly, to say something about the world, still less about the human condition. It is an aesthetic object complete in itself. It is not an instrument of any kind of humanism.

---

[1] Mark Edmundson, *Why Read?* (New York: Bloomsbury, 2004), 40–41.

[2] James Wood, *The Broken Estate: Essays on Literature and Belief* (New York: Picador, 1999), xx.

[3] Nathan A. Scott Jr., *Negative Capability: Studies in the New Literature and the Religious Situation* (New Haven, CT: Yale University Press, 1969), 10–11.

Evidently, these approaches to literature are challenges to the humanism of conventional realism and, indeed, to the way in which we have so far discussed literature and its relationship to the mysterious "matter" that lies beyond it. A blunter way to say this is that neither the postmodern critics nor the antiliterature proponents like Robbe-Grillet and Barthes believe that reading literature has anything at all to do with truth. Truth is a difficult concept and the achievement of absolute truth or even the full truth of anything may well be beyond us. Certainly, the truth of fiction and even more so of the poem is not fully graspable, and reading is a reaching out toward whatever the truth of this fiction or poem is, not its possession. As Edmundson argues, an interpretation cannot be measured by whether it is right or perfect, "but whether it leads us to a worldview that is potentially better than what we currently hold." "The gold standard," he adds, "is not epistemological perfection" but "the standard of use."[4] Robbe-Grillet, Barthes, and perhaps even Virginia Woolf would look blank at any suggestion that their works might be "useful," that they might somehow better an understanding of the human person or the world in which we live. Objectivity and practicality are neither their purpose nor what the reader finds in their fictions.

The Case for Neo-humanism

Neither Scott nor Wood nor Edmundson wishes to dismiss postmodern literature and literary theory as entirely valueless or destructive. Each is careful to nuance any criticism. Scott writes quite harshly of the poverty that befalls writers who make the decision for objectivity rather than realism or—its antithesis—myth. But he then proceeds to a more sympathetic explanation of what he continues to believe to be a futile purpose. If the twentieth century begins with the great novelists

[4] Edmundson, *Why Read?*, 55.

of modernity attempting to impose order on an increasingly disordered world, its second half shows much fiction abandoning that effort in the name of simply describing. Imposing order inevitably distorts that on which order has been imposed. Scott insists, however, that "there is no such thing as 'un-thought reality' " and consequently that the literature that attempts to describe before interpretation is destined to fail. "The world with which we have our actual transactions," he comments, "is never appropriable as something pristinely naked of human valuation."[5] James Wood offers an essentially similar judgment in his statement that "Barthes is right. . . . Or rather, he is right but *not quite* right." His mistake, as we noted above, is that in recognizing that fiction is exactly that, fictional, he jumps to the conclusion that "realism can never disclose the real." And if narrative is indeed only about itself, as Barthes would have it, "surely narrative can trade in effects without being always untrue."[6] And Donaldson, perhaps the most critical of the three when it comes to the impact of theory on reading, lays most of the blame at the feet of teachers, who invite students to apply theory without their having studied the theory itself. The result is that a student does not encounter Dickens's truth but "the truth according to Michel Foucault— or Fredric Jameson or Hélène Cixous." But he adds immediately that "it may be that the truths unfolded by Foucault and the rest are of consummate value . . ., are indispensable guides to life." "If so," he says, they "ought to be the objects of study in themselves."[7] The mistake is to take their terminology and interpose it between the reader and the text. As we might say in the language of our earlier discussions, such practices preclude the reader's capacity to attain the aesthetic object, which is a work of imagination, not of theory.

[5] Scott, *Negative Capability*, 61.
[6] Wood, *The Broken Estate*, 19.
[7] Edmundson, *Why Read?*, 39.

An even more nuanced critique of the impact of literary theory on humanism can be found in a 2004 article by Jens Zimmerman,[8] in which he argues that, while postmodern theory did overreach and has outlived its usefulness, its "insistence on the radically hermeneutical nature of human knowledge does not permit a simple return to old-fashioned humanism."[9] Nostalgia is "not helpful and may become dangerous," because good literature raises deep questions about human life, and "it is this desire for foundational questions concerning human existence that theory has in common with the best literature."[10] So the answer is to develop a "neo-humanism" that will not simply argue that reading books makes better people. These claims have to be examined, and so "the future of theory depends on a radical humanism based on a hermeneutic ontology."[11]

This very grand-sounding proposal in essence requires the recognition that interpretation does not follow close reading of texts but is always already present in the reading itself, because the reading is conducted by a reader who cannot ever be neutral. Moreover, the reader and the text and hence the frameworks of interpretation that we employ, consciously or not, are historically conditioned and constantly open to change. When we bring these two insights together we can imagine a newly understood humanism in which the human itself is not grasped unhistorically or with some ideologically inspired assumptions about the universality of "our" understanding of what it is to be human.

If the old humanism that was unhistorical and unaware of its ideological prejudices has to give way to neo-humanism, this means at the same time that all theory and the fictions that

---

[8] Jens Zimmerman, "*Quo Vadis?* Literary Theory beyond Postmodernism," *Christianity and Literature* 53, no. 4 (Summer 2004): 495–519.

[9] Ibid., 498.

[10] Ibid., 499.

[11] Ibid., 500.

are written in its light carry an understanding of what it is to be human as unavoidably as that of the great authors of the canon, and with the same capacity to overlook their own historicity and their own ideology. No text is ahistorical, and none is neutral. One cannot simply dismiss the more esoteric-sounding theory or the novels it generates because the world they imagine is not the one we wished we lived in, and one cannot dismiss conventional realism because of some assumption that it masks rather than reveals the objective world. All philosophy and all literature is generated by human beings, and what that which they are doing says about what it is to be a human being will always be what philosophy worries over and what literature depicts. There is no escaping it.

Is Religion about More Than Itself?

What do religion and the act of faith have to learn from the challenge to conventional realism offered in the name of post-modern theory and the resolution proposed in the name of neo-humanism? Puzzling our way through this question will require us to keep distinct the differences between religion and faith, as Dietrich Bonhoeffer would be the first to argue. An act of faith is evoked by an experience of the sacred, whether or not named as God or Christ, an act that puts the believer into a relationship with the sacred and orients that person's life toward a sense of presence and leads her or him to see life as the gift of the sacred. Religion is quite distinct, an altogether more earthbound matter. This difference is what so many younger souls are trying to express in the well-worn phrase, "I'm spiritual but not religious." While any religion is a vehicle for the transmission of a sense of its particular sacred through-out history, and a context in which ritual and communal wor-ship is most conveniently expressed, it does not guarantee faith in the sense in which we have just described it but tends toward requiring faith in the religious tradition itself as the way in which faith in its sacred ultimate reality is authenticated. Religion's greatest asset to the believer may be the support and confirmation offered by participation in a community of believers, just as its greatest temptation may be to allow the religious tradition itself to mediate, if not even control, the experience of the holy itself.

It seems fair to say that in practice the institutional face of Christianity and especially of Catholicism requires for its credibility that its adherents treat its claims as conventionally realistic. That is to say, they are presented and often enough appropriated as statements occasioned by a correspondence theory of truth. The propositions of religion—its doctrines in particular—are presented as if they correspond to what is objectively the case about God, Christ, salvation, the church, and so on. Though there is an apophatic element in Western Christianity, more so among the Eastern Orthodox, it is not stressed and it is not part of the spiritual world of most Christians. Church theology, when pressed, will grudgingly admit that statements about God do not in fact say anything objectively true about God, or at least that we do not know how they correspond to the divine reality, but hastily pass on to the language of revelation, language that is resolutely anthropomorphic and for the most part simply accepted as uncomplicatedly true by its adherents.

It seems likely that there is some relationship between the inattention to imagination in formal Christianity today and the decline of interest in participating in it. This is a tragedy, not least because the great doctrines of the tradition, of Trinity and incarnation in particular, have been and could again be the stimulus to enormous flights of the religious imagination. But as propositions proffered by religious institutions that seem to have lost their way, if not their place, in our world they no longer seem to point beyond themselves. The call to return to Scripture is a hopeful sign of the recognition that doctrines are little more than formalizations of the imaginative world of the Bible, but it will only work if reading Scripture frees the imagination, not if it must be filtered through the truth of doctrines that in fact depend on it.

Andrew Shanks offers us a useful way to think about this issue in his distinction between "the pathos of glory" and "the pathos of shakenness."[12] Shanks engages Julian Benda's distinction between two types of emotional need that can be met in politics or religion, that of pathos and that of ease.[13] Benda sees the need of pathos as tumultuous and dramatic, whereas the need of ease is gentle, calming, and conducive to meditation. But Shanks wants to dispute Benda's assumption that pathos is always in the end destructive and to be avoided by philosophers, hence the distinction between the pathos of glory and the pathos of shakenness. While the values contained in "ease" are not disputed, it is not correct, thinks Shanks, to identify the excitement of pathos solely negatively. Yes, there is a pathos of glory that is negative, identified as "an emotive celebration of values and aspirations serving the interests of power." But there is another version of pathos, "the pathos-laden celebration of high-principled dissent against popular, officially sanctioned prejudice." This is what Shanks calls "the pathos of shakenness," and it is this, rather than the pathos of glory, that contributes to the true purpose of religion, though formal religion is all too frequently found along the paths of the pathos of glory. Writing about the passion narrative in John's gospel, Shanks suggests that Pilate and the religious leaders "represent every sort of political or ethical establishment-mindedness . . . in perfect harmony with the

[12] Andrew Shanks, *What Is Truth? Towards a Theological Poetics* (London: Routledge, 2001).

[13] Benda is known today, if at all, for his 1927 book, *La trahison des clercs* (Paris: Grasset), translated into English as *The Treason of the Intellectuals* (New York: Morrow, 1928). But Shanks primarily references an earlier work, *Mon Premier Testament*, published in Paris in 1911 by Les Cahiers de la Quinzaine and reprinted in 1928 by Gallimard.

perceived self-interest of those in power."[14] Jesus, on the contrary, proclaims "the good news inherent in the symbolic overthrow of all establishment-mindedness." This is "the gospel of shakenness," but because Jesus is shown as a model of "perfect inner calm," what we see in the gospel is the "special juxtaposition of the most intense pathos of shakenness with a portrayal of perfect serenity."[15]

Shanks's distinctions are useful in the analysis of the weakening impact of "organized" or formal religion today, especially Catholicism. It may be that its establishment-mindedness blunts dissent for the simple reason that it knows that imagination is freedom. The perfect example of this stand-off is the conversation between Jesus and the Grand Inquisitor in Dostoevsky's *The Brothers Karamazov*. The Inquisitor represents the church that has given people what they want, the spiritual sloth of empty comfort, rather than the fearsome prospect of following Jesus wherever the imagination takes them. The mix of genuine serenity and freedom from fear is what Jesus represents, "the reality of a freedom beyond the systems of the world," in Rowan Williams's words,[16] especially when Jesus' response to the long-winded self-justification of the Inquisitor is a simple kiss on his bloodless lips. Appropriately enough, Dostoevsky depicts the Inquisitor's church as an elite company of unbelievers devoted to promoting a faith of false consciousness among the masses. There is no need to see this as a one-to-one correspondence to the structures of institutional Catholicism to find aspects of it enlightening. Doctrinally speaking, Catholicism is a religion of centralized control, though surveys of American Catholicism in particular show that this control is fast evaporating, *even among those who continue to consider themselves Catholic and who continue to attend*

---

[14] Shanks, *What Is Truth?*, 14.

[15] Ibid., 15.

[16] Rowan Williams, *Dostoevsky: Language, Faith and Fiction* (Waco, TX: Baylor University Press, 2011), 31.

church, though often less frequently than in the past.[17] These surveys show on the whole a pattern of growing insistence on thinking for oneself. It would be quite accurate to understand this as the believer interpreting the text and forming in the imagination, in the space between the text and the reader, a religious object that corresponds in high degree to Iser's aesthetic object. It may also be the case that the sacred, the "matter" behind the text which we can never wholly grasp, is common to both the doctrinal authority and the believer who interprets.

That the "same God" is worshiped by the more independent Catholic of today and the formal tradition that continues to try to insist on much that is not open to interpretation is proven in the evidence that surveys provide that much "dissent" is contained within a continuing attachment to the church, particularly to its liturgy. Dissenters still communicate. And if dissenters are comfortable with this situation, it is also the case that they have felt less "outside" the mainstream of the church under the pontificate of Pope Francis than for many years previous. The struggles of Pope Francis to turn the church back to the Gospel and—dare we say it—further from the law are a textbook example of the confrontation between the pathos of glory and the pathos of shakenness. That this need not result in breakdown of communication between the two approaches, or even schism, depends on the degree to which both recognize that either pathos must be accompanied by the "need for ease," which has its perfect exemplar in the serenity of Jesus Christ. Prayer, that of the dissenters and that of the establishment, is the missing ingredient in ecclesial confrontations.

A church inspired by the pathos of shakenness will be a countercultural force, marked by a very particular understanding of truth. As Andrew Shanks asks, while there is meaning to the notion of truth as correctness, is it not the case that

[17] See William V. D'Antonio, Michele Dillon, and Mary L. Gautier, *American Catholics in Transition* (Lanham, MD: Rowman & Littlefield, 2013).

there must be some prior disposition that allows us to recognize the persuasiveness of any proposition? And is not this "initial predisposition of readiness, already as such, itself an embodiment of truth?" The truth that precedes science, ethics, and metaphysics is "the original turning of the will to genuine thoughtfulness," or "truth-as-honesty." For Shanks, this kind of predisposition can either remain quite subliminal or it can be given expression "in the sheer pathos-laden evocativeness of truthful poetry."[18] It can also, we may want to argue, be evident in the imagination of the reader approaching serious fiction, even and perhaps especially in the mode of the subliminal or unconscious. In the aesthetic object the reader's imagination is engaged with the text in the space between the two, but the aesthetic is only mysteriously connected to the matter. In the act of faith that for a Christian is the product of the encounter between the self and Christ as other in a space that is not the self and not Christ, the faith-product orients the believer to the holy that lies beyond all human comprehension, the mystery of God, the "matter" that is the meaning of the whole.

We can then conclude that religion that does not promote and inspire the use of the imagination is religion that impedes faith. To the degree that it does so, it is simply about itself, not about faith in the holy that lies beyond it. Too much of formal religion claims more than it can possibly know, and at times seems to set rules that not only delimit the adherent's range of possibilities but also operate as if it, and not the Holy Spirit, is in charge. The freedom of the Spirit and the freedom of the individual believer's religious imagination are not high on the priority list of the doctrinal or moral traditions of the church. If the tradition moves forward and if there is genuine develop-

---

[18] Shanks, *What Is Truth?*, 16–17.

ment of doctrine in the church,[19] which can hardly be denied, it is often and rightly said to occur through the voice of the whole church or the *sensus fidelium*. What is perhaps not so often noticed is that this sense of the faithful is a flow of acts of the religious imagination. The virtue of hope is itself pure imagination.

If it is correct that the current weakness of Western religion in general and Catholicism in particular is a result of the failure to encourage imagination, then whatever feeds the imaginative power of the believer, whatever nourishes faith, will be support to the individual and, perhaps more important, a source of strength to a religious tradition in serious need of new sources of energy. Here, in the end, is where the arts in general and fiction in particular have profound therapeutic potential. If we are convinced by Henry James's description of "the matter" that lies beyond the text, beyond the author's grasp and the reader's total comprehension, then we can even say that serious literature is always a kind of theological reflection, even when it is ostensibly far from what we would consider to be the usual patterns of religious thought. We may even be able to maintain this for literature that deliberately sets out to avoid any sense that it means anything beyond itself. Maybe even Robbe-Grillet. Perhaps Virginia Woolf. Whatever stimulates the imagination moves the reader into the formation of an aesthetic object whose implicit and often subliminal end point is a vision of the whole. And even a nihilistic work of fiction can be grist to the mill of the religious imagination, so long as its power is in stimulating the imagination and so long as it resists mere didacticism. Which is, of course, equally true for a fiction written with religious perceptions or overtones. If a work of fiction is not a space for the imagination, it is not

[19] See here the magisterial work of John E. Thiel, *Senses of Tradition: Continuity and Development in Catholic Faith* (New York: Oxford University Press, 2000).

serious fiction in the sense in which we are using the term. If it is didactic—religious or atheistic—it is not worth our time. If it is what Graham Greene would classify as "an entertainment," it is just that. It entertains us for a time, and then we move on, unchanged.

James Wood's Critique of Religion

One of the finest of today's literary critics, James Wood, has devoted much of his best work to exploring what has happened to the sense of the sacred in Western literature over the past two hundred years.[20] In the introduction to *The Broken Estate* Wood distinguishes fiction as "the place of not-quite-belief" from religion, which, if it "is true, one must believe." Arguing that literary and religious belief are distinctly different, Wood recognizes that from the mid-nineteenth century onward the distinctions became less clear, with the gospels beginning to be read as fictional tales and fiction becoming "an almost religious activity." Flaubert stands for the movement "to turn literary style into a religion," while Ernest Renan begins to turn religion "into a kind of style, a poetry." A number of the texts he discusses, says Wood, "pace the limits of the 'not-quite,' in both fiction and religion."[21] Some of the earlier essays, in particular, take up this task. So, for example, we see Austen described as a key moment in the development of interiority in the novel. A wonderful essay on Melville draws a picture of him as one who replaces God with the creativity of metaphor, which must inevitably lead to the dismissal of the "Original Author." Flaubert appears as one who portends the modern novel's shift to appearances only, that is, away

[20] In particular in *The Broken Estate: Essays on Literature and Belief* (New York: Picador, 1999, 2010) and, more recently, in *The Nearest Thing to Life* (Waltham, MA: Brandeis, 2015).

[21] Wood, *The Broken Estate*, xxi.

from the deliberate exploration of meaning. Chekhov invents "free consciousness," where the inner life that is free "bumps up against" the mundane outer life. And Virginia Woolf sees the whole world as a work of art, where the art behaves like ritual, not doctrine, ornamenting what cannot be known. As Woolf put it, "I'm certain that the only meanings that are worth anything in a work of art are those that the artist himself knows nothing about." This may seem to us to have echoes of Henry James's notion of "the matter" that lies behind the work of art, Coleridge's primary imagination. Wood recognizes that there is a mystical element in Woolf's work, especially in *To the Lighthouse* and *The Waves*, but rightly classifies it as secular mysticism. That which is hinted at here, that which is unspoken and even unknown, is not God, whatever it is.

The final chapter of *The Broken Estate* steps back from the topic of literature. Here Wood explores how nineteenth-century thinkers like Renan and Arnold reduce religion to a human creation principally directed toward a moral purpose, when religion's strength can only be in its truth. If religion is true and salvation is its prize, then it is supremely valuable. As an atheist, Wood cannot accept religion, criticizing both those thinkers who reduce religion to something other than truth and religion for its lack of truth. His personal testimony is to a preference for a false purpose invented by human beings, not by God, and therefore that "one can strip it away to reveal the *actual* pointlessness" of life.[22] This is a very bleak picture and a surprising one for someone who can write so beautifully of the works of fiction. Is he just whiling away his time? If there were a God, he concludes, "why must we move through this unhappy, painful, rehearsal for heaven, this desperate antechamber, this foreword written by an anonymous author, this hard prelude in which so few of us can find our way?"[23] But

[22] Ibid., 261.
[23] Ibid., 270.

without God, it would seem, this must be exactly what the world is. So what exactly are the great authors doing, and why?

It would be a foolish reader who would take issue with Wood's judgments on literature, but he may not be the best authority on the nature of religion. The authors he discusses in *The Broken Estate* are sensitively examined and his conclusions are invariably enlightening. His views on Renan, Arnold, Paul Johnson, Richard Swinburne, and Don Cupitt seem entirely valid, and the claim that with the intent of saving religion they have undermined it is quite persuasive. Where there is reason to doubt his conclusions and consequently space to disagree is in the picture he paints of what religion, specifically the Christian religion, actually claims to be. And if he is wrong about this, then it may be that he is wrong to see religion and literature as two entirely different kinds of belief.

Wood's upbringing in evangelical and charismatic Anglicanism, by his own account, is a black-and-white affair. Even if he does not believe any longer, "the child of evangelicalism . . . inherits nevertheless a suspicion of indifference." Such a one who rejects the religion he grew up with "rejects it religiously."[24] So fiction as the "game of not-quite-belief" is importantly different from religion: "Fiction asks us to judge its reality; religion asserts its reality." Without making invidious comparisons between religious traditions, compare this to Patricia Hampl's comment that "in my romantic Catholic upbringing the line between literature and religion was always airily imprecise."[25] It seems likely that Wood might accept this judgment from the side of literature, since his essays in *The Broken Estate* mostly tread the imprecise line between fiction and religion, but he would surely reject it from the side of religion. If religion is not clear about how it is different from

[24] Ibid., 256.
[25] Patricia Hampl, *Blue Arabesque: A Search for the Sublime* (New York: Harcourt, 2006), 87.

literature, then it falls prey to the Renans and Arnolds and Cupitts of this world, who would save it by interpreting it in literary terms.

Where Wood seems to go wrong is in his confusion of religion and faith, on the one hand, and, on the other, his determinedly literalist reading of the gospels. To the first confusion it is necessary to insist that believers put their faith in religion at their peril. Their faith is in the God who lies beyond religion, whereas the religion through which they may approach God is exactly that, a way of approach to a reality whose truth lies beyond the framework of religion. To the second confusion we have to be clear that, on the one hand, one cannot simply read the gospels as a straightforward account of the words and deeds of Jesus and, on the other, that Christian faith in Jesus is gospel-bound in the sense that scriptural faith requires an act of trust in the picture of Jesus presented by the evangelists. Faith in this sense is a faith in the trustworthiness of the tradition, albeit that the tradition provides four interpretations of a figure who is not accessible through any texts other than the gospels. Wood is wrong to be dismissive of Oscar Wilde's description of the gospels as "four prose-poems about Christ." This is exactly what they are.[26] Faith in that other sense, which we discussed in the early chapters, is a personal, even mystical relationship that the individual believer has with God in and through Jesus Christ. Both this faith and the scriptural faith as trust in the tradition are maintained by the believer to be true, even ultimately true, though *how* they are true is in the end shrouded in mystery.

James Wood is not a theologian, though he is a very insightful observer of things religious, but the importance of his imprecision on issues of faith is that it sheds light on a rather closer connection between works of fiction and works of faith than he seems to recognize—and perhaps than he would be

[26] See Wood, *The Broken Estate*, 250.

willing to admit. It is highly likely that he would resist treating the gospels as literary texts, because as he so rightly says the "as-if" of fiction is not applicable in the context of religion. At the same time, however, we need to insist that the gospel texts possess both a measure of ambiguity and the surplus of meaning that is the mark of serious fiction. Were it not so, there would be no preachers drawing out the meanings of the text, because there would be nothing beyond the plain sense of the words. Strict fundamentalism or biblical literalism aside, no believer thinks that the text simply says what it says. It is, to borrow words from Frank Kermode on the characteristics of a classic, "possessed of a plurality of ambiguities enlarged by the action of time."[27] To build a faith relationship to Jesus Christ is entirely analogous to developing the aesthetic object in reading fiction. The believer has appropriated the texts of the tradition in the space between him or her and in an act of the imagination has encountered the person of Christ. One might say that the person of Christ is the "religious object," structurally akin to the aesthetic object but different in much the way Wood suggests, affirmed as ultimately true, not simply as-if true. But the similarity goes a little further than this. The encounter with Christ is not a literal encounter, any more than the aesthetic object has actual concreteness. Both occur in the imagination, which is not to say that either is imaginary. Moreover, both point beyond themselves: the aesthetic object to the "matter" or mystery that lies beyond it; the religious object to the mysterious God who is beyond human comprehension.

There is no question that Wood is correct to chart the challenges of waning religious belief through the texts of nineteenth- and twentieth-century fiction, though the interpretation he puts on it is not the only possibility. The selection of authors in *The Broken Estate* has been made to substantiate this point. One could imagine another set of texts of compa-

---

[27] Frank Kermode, *The Classic* (London: Faber & Faber, 1975), 133.

rable literary quality that might suggest a different picture: Dostoevsky and Tolstoy from the nineteenth century, Flannery O'Connor and Muriel Spark and Marilynne Robinson from the twentieth. On the whole, the weight of evidence is on his side but open to more than one interpretation. From the perspective of a Christian theology of grace, there is no work of the imagination that is not in some sense a search for the sacred, and there is no reading of serious fiction that does not in some sense confront the subject with the possibility of a depth of meaning beyond what the surface meaning of the text seems to be. This is surely what lies behind Simone Weil's remark that "all art of the highest order is religious in essence."[28]

"Anatheism"

James Wood's account of the state of faith in the sacred can be further enriched by considering it on the axis of faith and doubt. There is no better recent place for this examination than in Richard Kearney's book, *Anatheism*,[29] which issues a direct challenge to Wood's prevailing assumption that faith or its opposite are in the end the only two options. What Kearney leads us to contemplate is what people of faith by and large know anyway, that faith in today's world is possessed with a certain amount of frailty, often mixed with doubt and not infrequently very close to the "not-quite-belief" that for Wood is the distinctive mark of fiction. The reduction of religion to something like story, which Wood outlines in the final chapter of *The Broken Estate*, is rightly to be dismissed as well-meaning capitulation to the spirit of the times. But the enlistment of literature to the cause of enlarging the religious imagination's understanding of how faith can be possessed tenuously, if not

[28] Simone Weil, *Gravity and Grace* (Omaha, NE: Bison Books, 1997), 207.
[29] Richard Kearney, *Anatheism: Returning to God after God* (New York: Columbia University Press, 2010).

provisionally, is quite another matter. To recognize secular mysticism is surely the antithesis of a rationalizing or moralizing religion.

Kearney proposes a third way beyond the two poles of "dogmatic theism" and "militant atheism," which he designates "anatheism" or belief in "God after God." While we have no right to put words into the mouth of anyone, it is not hard to imagine the James Wood of *The Broken Estate* consigning this idea to the category of less than authentic religious belief. But what should stop him short, if indeed he would respond in this way, is that in fact this third way is where the vast majority of people living in formerly Christian cultures actually reside in today's world, on a spectrum somewhere between a questioning embrace of the Christian tradition and a recognition, as Hannah Arendt has argued, that both belief and nonbelief are suffused with doubt. "Our world is a spiritually secular world," she wrote, "precisely because it is a world of doubt."[30] But one can also turn this around and proclaim that the world is spiritually religious for precisely the same reason. Faith is never absolutely certain about anything. The Christian mystical tradition shows countless examples of how faith and doubt are inextricably intermingled and indeed how faith can sometimes seem quite blasphemous. Meister Eckhart's "deny God for God's sake" is simply one striking example of how religious belief cannot be constrained within the kind of "religion" that the new atheists inveigh so inaccurately against.

Some of Wood's more recent writings show either a modified or clarified statement of his position on religion. This is particularly true of an essay based on the first of the Weidenfeld Lectures delivered in Oxford in 2011, titled "The Modern Novel

---

[30] Hannah Arendt, "Religion and Politics" in *Essays in Understanding*, ed. Jerome Kohn (New York: Harcourt Brace Jovanovich, 1994), 369, quoted in Kearney, *Anatheism*, 59.

and the New Atheism."[31] Here he argues, as Terry Eagleton and others have done before him, that the more celebrated new atheists like Richard Dawkins and Christopher Hitchens are in fact arguing against the God of the nineteenth century. He remains as frankly contemptuous of dogmatic evangelical religion, particularly its American variants, as he was in the earlier book, but he is much more willing to recognize that religious belief today takes many other more sophisticated forms. Dawkins and the others are not wrong to attack religion, but they are wrong to think that they are attacking religion when in fact they are attacking one variant of it that had its heyday long ago, though it survives in fundamentalist American Christianity today. "I would rather," writes Wood, "that the New Atheists refrained from speculation altogether than plunge into their flimsy anthropological-quasi-neuroscientific-evolutionary-biological kitbags." The New Atheism "offers feeble accounts of why people believe in God" and "feeble accounts of secular intellectual history." It combats biblical literalism with its own brand of literalism. Wood's alternative suggestion is "that the modern novel . . . offers a space within which we might be able to explore some contemporary theological issues." Mark Edmundson, as we saw, held much the same opinion and saw this as his primary justification for beginning the study of literature by approaching religious questions. The addition on which we need to insist is that exactly because Wood and Edmundson are correct in their assessment, we can also claim that these works of fiction may actually enrich the contemporary *religious* imagination, making it sturdier than it otherwise might be while not removing its distinctly anatheistic posture.

Kearney addresses precisely this issue in his discussion of what he calls "a sacramental experience of the everyday" to

[31] Available currently only online at www.abc.net.au/religion/articles/2011/07/04/3259863.htm.

be found in the work of contemporary agnostic philosophers like Maurice Merleau-Ponty and Julia Kristeva and the application of the "sacramental poetics" he elaborates there to the work of novelists, among whom he singles out Joyce, Proust, and Woolf. From the secular side of things, Merleau-Ponty is key, though for an atheist he was fairly Catholic in his sympathies and he had a profound understanding of what the late-lamented Andrew Greeley liked to call the sacramental imagination.[32] Merleau-Ponty disliked the choice between beings and Being. To him "flesh" or the body was the mediator between the two. In one way this seems quite traditional. From a religious perspective one could think, as Catholics do, that any aspect of the world can direct us to the creator God who lies beyond. From a secular perspective, embodied reality or "flesh" is the presence of mystery. But Merleau-Ponty treated this idea anything but traditionally. For him, the flesh is not matter so much as it is the meeting point between the individual and the Idea or, as a Christian might say, the world is the place of the encounter with the Word made flesh. Theologically, Merleau-Ponty's vision is radically kenotic. "God" is emptied out into history, the transcendent is present *only* in the immanent (this is his atheistic moment) and "God needs human history" (this is the religious moment). There is an atheistic moment in Christianity, symbolized in Christ's cry of despair on Golgotha. As Kearney concludes, "By relocating transcendence in the immanence of nature, Merleau-Ponty is restoring logos to the flesh of the world."[33] Or in its more prosaic form, "The sacrament of transubstantiation is to the responsive communicant what the sensible is to the capable perceiver."[34]

---

[32] Above all, see his *The Catholic Imagination* (Berkeley: University of California Press, 2000).

[33] Kearney, *Anatheism*, 94.

[34] Ibid., 89.

To the Lighthouse

Virginia Woolf's finest novel, *To the Lighthouse*, offers us an opportunity to test the way in which a person of faith can read creatively even the most secular of fictions. This does *not* mean that her novel is clandestinely religious or "about" the sacred. The integrity of this work lies in Woolf's determination not to have the fiction be about anything but itself. Frankly, it is not really *about* anything, other than the thoughts that flit through the minds of the various characters living in a summer home on the Isle of Skye at two moments separated by the Great War. Like Lily Briscoe, the guest who is also an amateur painter, Woolf is creating a picture, but the picture is the composite of the thoughts of a number of the characters in the story, into which the narrator rarely intrudes herself. Reading the book, we are almost always tracking the shifting thoughts of one character, seeing things through his or her eyes, including the other characters in the story. There is absolutely no effort, indeed there is a deliberate intent not to comment in any authorial way on the meaning of it all and not to privilege one sensibility rather than another, not even that of Mrs. Ramsay, though it is clearly her consciousness and the remembrance of her presence that dominate the entire work.

To the Lighthouse is like nothing so much as a fictional counterpart to impressionist painting, the landscapes of Monet, the human figures of Manet, and the deliberately imprecise lines of the *pointilliste* Seurat. While the painters depict the outsides of their subjects in such a way as to hint at something of what is going on within them, Woolf depicts the insides of her characters, though often enough through elaborate descriptions of how they are perceiving their physical surroundings. And if there were a soundtrack to the novel, one would expect to hear not so much the voices of the players, since little enough is said throughout the story, but more likely in the first part of the text music redolent of languid summer days in Edwardian England, strangely enough perhaps French music like Debussy's

Petite Suite: En bateau, to be replaced in the third part with Mendelssohn's Hebrides overture, *Fingal's Cave,* recalling the turbulence of the trip to the Lighthouse, perhaps separated by Britten's War Requiem, which set much of Wilfrid Owen's war poetry to music. The music paints a picture that is emotionally compelling and visually imprecise. The novel does likewise, composed as it is of scattered thoughts and impressions that tell a story of memory, loss, love, elegy, and—above all—the capacity of art to hint at something beneath the surface of what we see around us. Like impressionism in music and painting, Virginia Woolf works through suggestion and the creation of atmosphere. She doesn't so much tell a story as communicate feelings and moods, inviting us into a sensibility that reshapes the reader's perceptions.

The first of the three parts of *To the Lighthouse* takes place in the space of one day in the high Edwardian era before the First World War, at a shabby summer home on the Isle of Skye occupied by an academic philosopher and his wife, their eight children, and an assortment of their guests, including a second academic, an elderly poet, a middle-aged amateur painter, and a poor graduate student whom the children unkindly have dubbed "the little atheist." As the book begins the six-year-old James is sitting with his mother, Mrs. Ramsay, having his hopes dashed about a possible boat trip to the offshore lighthouse by his unnecessarily cruel father and his sycophantic graduate student. Mrs. Ramsay's thoughts are our only access to this set of events and to the rest of the day that follows, climaxing with a glorious scene of everyone gathered around the dinner table. Who loves and who hates? Who is happy and who is not? Is Mrs. Ramsay as beautiful on the inside as she is physically? Or is she manipulative and conventional? Do she and her husband love one another or not, and what is such a love anyway? What will the future bring for the Ramsay children? Will Mrs. Ramsay succeed in engineering an engagement between two of the younger guests, and should she be trying?

All these and more reflections go through her mind as the day progresses, and as she leaves the room at the end of the final dinner scene, a moment that she had felt "partook of eternity," she looks back to see that "it had become . . . already the past."

The brief middle section of the book, "Time Passes," carries us over the next ten years, years that include the Great War in which one of the children is killed in battle. Mrs. Ramsay also dies "off stage" as it were, and her daughter Prue—the most beautiful of the children—dies just a few months after her marriage. For one reason or another the family does not return to the house for ten years, and the house declines and comes close to dereliction before they decide finally to return, ushering in the third section, again occupying the space of less than a day, in which Mr. Ramsay finally takes two of the younger children—James and Cam, now teenagers—to the lighthouse. In this third section the cast of characters is smaller but the reflections are shared out a little more, about half to Lily Briscoe as she works on a painting in the garden of the house, and Cam as she makes the boat trip to the lighthouse. This third section is both elegiac, reflecting on all that once was and is now lost, and oriented more clearly to a resolution that Mrs. Ramsay's thoughts never considered. Lily has been following the progress of the boating party and concludes, "He has landed. . . . It is finished." And turning to her painting she adds the one line that she believes pulls everything together, thinking "It was done; it was finished," and commenting in the last words of the novel, "I have had my vision."

To the Lighthouse has much to offer to the religious imagination. In the first instance, the complex emotions of a character trying to bring order to her consciousness despite the disorder of the relationships she considers important has its parallel in the negative capability of any person of faith's appropriation of meaning, always held in tension with doubt. Recall James Wood's classification of literature as the "not-quite-belief," but remember too our distinction between faith and religion.

"Faith" is distinctly closer to the not-quite-belief of fiction than it is to the hard certainties of religion. Sometimes a lighthouse is just a lighthouse, but in the first part of the story it also serves as the unattainable object of desire, reached in part 3 when Ramsay stands in the boat as it approaches the shore, "for all the world, James thought, as if he were saying: 'There is no God,'" as he sprang, "lightly like a young man, holding his parcel, on to the rock." The godless rock on which he stands is identified by the old poet Mr. Carmichael, standing beside Lily Briscoe, as the final destiny of "all the weakness and suffering of mankind." Turning from him, Lily in a moment of "sudden intensity" completes her painting. Life's pagan achievement on the godless rock is surpassed by the creative accomplishment of the artist. Where there is no God, there is art.

A person whose faith is shaped by the Christian tradition experiences God, the object of that faith, in a manner on which Woolf's novel sheds considerable light. Even the great saints and mystics would lay claim to direct experience of God, if at all, in brief moments. Mostly, faith is in a God who is glimpsed in encounters with other people or in moments of appreciation and wonder at the beauties of the natural world or the creativity of great artists. In *To the Lighthouse* these same glimpses of human goodness, natural beauty, and artistic creativity lead Mrs. Ramsay or Lily Briscoe toward some nameless beyond, to some lighthouse in the mind, which to them is not God, though what it is they are not sure. There is a famous passage in which Mrs. Ramsay, in a moment of quiet, reflects on how one does not find rest in the self but freedom and peace in the dark immensity of all we do not know. Each of us is "a wedge of darkness" who must step aside from all our attachments and focus on one thing, in her case on the beam of light from the lighthouse. "Often she found herself sitting and looking," she thought, "until she became the thing she looked at," and as she turns to the idea that everything will end, "suddenly she added: We are in the hands of the Lord." Of course she is both confused and furious with herself to have come out with that trite religious sentiment. There is no reason, order and justice in the world, she thinks, but only "suffering, death, the poor."[35]

The believer and Mrs. Ramsay may very well go through the same quasi-mystical sense of resting upon a mystery too great to fathom, which somehow comforts and assures. But the difference between their responses to these common experiences is one of apperception in the sense in which William James employs the term:

> Every impression that comes in from without, be it a sentence which we hear, an object of vision, or an effluvium which assails our nose, no sooner enters our consciousness than it is drafted off in some determinate direction or other, making connection with the other materials already there, and finally producing what we call our reaction.[36]

It is apperception that makes the exactly similar experience lead one person to say with sincerity that we are in the hands of the Lord and another to reject the idea of such dependence. Everything that enters our consciousness is placed in relationship to what is already there. A believer may cry with Gerard Manley Hopkins, "glory be to God for dappled things," and Mrs. Ramsay could glory in the same without giving God the gratitude. But what we learn from *To the Lighthouse* that is so valuable is not only that Mrs. Ramsay has to take account of the impulsive resting in the hands of the Lord but also that Virginia Woolf herself wanted to lay out before us the complexity of human consciousness, even that which might claim to be atheistic—as she surely did—in which there is a depth, a darkness perhaps, but a something that is not ourselves on which our own sense of our self somehow rests. When Lily

[35] How interesting Bonhoeffer would have found this remark!
[36] "Talks to Teachers," in *William James: Writing, 1878–1899*, The Library of America (New York: Penguin Putnam, 1992), 801.

Briscoe paints in the final line on her painting and pronounces an ending, to the work and the book, she adds in "extreme fatigue" that she has had her vision. Not a religious vision of course, still less a vision of God, but a vision of the tremendous beauty of the whole of what there is, a vision with which the believer can surely sympathize.

Faith is tentative if not provisional, religion is positive, often falsely so, and *To the Lighthouse* creates a world in which the person of faith can feel at home. Love, folly, art, and experience are the components of a full life behind which lies a mystery, one which—like the lighthouse—is always present, shedding light, though for the most part we do not notice it, but whose full reality is tantalizingly just beyond reach. In this world the faithful person is warned against overreaching. Faith is not the possession of absolute mystery so much as the confidence that it is somehow there and that we feel its effects in our time of trial as surely as the light from the lighthouse illuminates the darkness. Moreover, the person of faith inhabits the same experiences as the agnostic or atheist and to a high degree shares the feelings. The trust or confidence comes from who knows where, and it is possessed humbly, not broadcast proudly, if only because faith is shadowed by doubt. Some days, we are all Mrs. Ramsay.

Books like *To the Lighthouse* in the end serve as therapy for the religious imagination of today, though they do so only insofar as they are read and appreciated for their own authenticity, not because they are susceptible to some sort of crude translation into religious metaphors. Virginia Woolf's novel reveals a sensibility that struggles with the profound issues of love, loss, death, and memory in a way that any sensitive intelligence can appreciate and that should feel no different because the reader is a person of faith. The problems of life and the questions of ultimacy that flutter in the background of any reflective person are not different because one is a believer or one is not. Or if they are, then the way the religious believer treats them, when he or she steps beyond trust and hope into confident certainty, teeters on the brink of inauthenticity and bids fair to depart in some serious way from the normal human condition of everyday life. The religious and the literary imagination both reach out tentatively toward a grasp of the whole that inevitably escapes total possession. When the religious imagination escapes into fancy and paints mental pictures of life in heaven or the spirit-world of guardian angels, it does no harm so long as such fancies rest on the certain knowledge that the truth in which we trust escapes our comprehension. *To the Lighthouse* is full of fancy, but built on the dimly held awareness of something beyond and beneath the everyday, something hinted at in the daily flicker of loving moments or in the artist's struggle toward completion.

There are multiple causes of the impoverishment of today's religious imagination. Some of them are cultural, others more narrowly religious. A culture focused on possession imperils the capacity for self-possession, while a culture of desire frustrates the ability to be present, and present to self. Forgetting the past, in our day the present moment is too often simply the take-off point for desiring into the future. If noise is all around us, how can we be quiet, and if we are in constant motion, how difficult becomes simple awareness of the beauty of the present and the presence of mystery. These characteristics of our culture infect the religious imagination because people of faith are also products of our culture, sharing in its strengths and weaknesses. For most of today's Catholics, religious rituals are less than rich; prayer is squeezed into busy lives when possible, if at all; the community of faith is concrete for an hour a week; and the art and music that surrounds us at worship is pallid at best, sometimes plainly kitschy.[37]

---

[37] Do not mistake these words as a yearning for the lost mystifications of the Latin Mass, but do understand them as a call for a way to find how we can restore in today's experience of liturgy and prayer some of what we discarded when we rightly proclaimed that liturgy requires "full, conscious and active participation" of the whole body of the faithful.

One way to draw together the religious and the literary imaginations is to dwell on the fashionable notion of mindfulness and to recognize that simplification of life is a necessary precondition for its cultivation. This if nothing else is the enduring legacy of the monastic life, in that sense always countercultural. Our culture is not mindful. Faith should make us mindful. Good literature encourages mindfulness. But routine religion is anything but mindful, and most people these days don't read the kind of books that promote mindfulness. Mindfulness does not lead to a person being religious rather than atheistic, or vice-versa, and it does not lead someone to liberal or conservative conclusions on the great issues of life. Resurrection or reincarnation may be the conclusion of equally mindful people. The systematic application of reflection to the challenges of living humanely in our world, however, especially today, has to look beyond greedy consumption and see the connection between living wisely and the future of our planet. Good literature can push the atheist or the believer in much the same direction.

Chapter Six

What's Catholicism Got to Do with It?

Sacred and Secular Scriptures

While for the most part the word "faith" can be employed to designate the approach to life of all religious people and can be contrasted to a more secular set of convictions, it is clear that the incarnational beliefs of the Christian tradition in its Catholic form lead to its being significantly distinctive in its approach to the secular world. Those traditions that believe the world is the creation of a good God inevitably value the created world. But if God becomes human, then in the Catholic understanding—still more among the Orthodox—humanity carries traits of divinity, and to some degree the place and role of the human race in the world mirrors something of the relationship the creator God has to this world. To be created in the image and likeness of God, as the book of Genesis puts it, is not to be like God in appearance, for God has no appearance. It is rather to be like God in God's creativity and purpose in creation, and while we cannot confidently explain divine purposiveness, we can certainly infer from the creation of the world something at least of what this means about the creator. If God is love, as the Christian tradition understands, then since love must expand beyond itself, must be poured out if it is anything more than self-love—even trinitarian self-love—then creation is the self-expression of the God who is love. To be made in the image and likeness of God is to be charged with the task of loving, above all, loving the world that God made as a home for us and all living things.

The Catholic religious imagination is often referred to as a sacramental imagination, precisely because the particular way that the Catholic tradition understands the creation/incarnation relationship leads to the belief that everything in the created order can be a means of encountering the divine. Nothing in creation is of itself excluded from sacramentality, though anything in creation can be perverted from its truth. One of the most striking paradoxes of creation theology is that it is the one being about whom the tradition says it is "made in the image and likeness of God," that is responsible for any and every perversion of the natural order's sacramentality. Nevertheless, if it is a case of overweening anthropocentrism to see human beings as the crown of creation, it is quite correct to see us as the consciousness of creation, at least for the present, since we do not know where the evolutionary process will lead. The paradise that was the home of Adam and Eve would, without them, be a paradise known only to God.

Fiction, whether its authors or readers know it or not, exists within this sacramental universe. And serious fiction, even that which is written by atheists or even for the purpose of undermining religious faith and promoting secularity, insofar as it strives to reveal truth, somehow reveals something of God. From the perspective of faith there can be no separation between God and truth, and that which is true is thereby godly. God is in the truth and the truth is in God, and in neither case does it mean the reduction of the religious to the secular or the forced canonization of what is authentically secular. This is surely something of what Flannery O'Connor meant by her insistence that imposing orthodoxy on fiction is impossible. "Our sense of what is contained in our faith," she wrote, "is deepened less by abstractions than by an encounter with mystery in what is human and often perverse." She argued that Catholics like "the instant answer" and fiction doesn't have any. The fiction writer, she thought, does something akin to Scripture: "Saint Gregory wrote that every time the sacred text describes a fact, it reveals a mystery. And this is what the fiction writer, on his lower level, attempts to do also."[1]

The Cambridge professor Nicholas Boyle offers a valuable discussion of this relationship between what he calls "sacred and secular scriptures."[2] Boyle argues that a Catholic approach to literature must find a way between two sets of views espoused by Friedrich Schleiermacher and Paul Ricoeur. First, on the matter of revelation, there is Schleiermacher's position that Scripture records the history of revelations made to individuals in the past, countered by Ricoeur's view that the Bible is revelatory now, but so are all other literary texts. Second, with regard to questions of intention, while Schleiermacher is famously committed to recovering the intention of the author in any hermeneutical inquiry, Ricoeur opposes such an approach, favoring instead the intention revealed by the text. The Catholic approach, says Boyle, will seek to reconcile the two opposing perspectives. It will distinguish sacred writings controlled by a hermeneutic of revelation from secular writings controlled by a hermeneutic of authorship, but it will recognize overlap. To some degree the Bible has to be open to historicist literary criticism, and some secular literature is capable "of rising to a meaning that can only be elucidated by theological exegesis."[3]

The heart of Boyle's argument insofar as it relates to our principal concerns is found in his statement that, from a Catholic perspective that includes both sacred and secular texts, "literature is language free of instrumental purpose, and

---

[1] From "The Catholic Novelist in the South," in *Flannery O'Connor: Collected Works*, The Library of America (New York: Penguin Putnam, 1988), 863.

[2] Nicholas Boyle, *Sacred and Secular Scriptures: A Catholic Approach to Literature* (Notre Dame, IN: University of Notre Dame Press, 2005).

[3] Ibid., 120.

it seeks to tell the truth."[4] This nonpurposive character of sacred and secular literature is what makes them both potentially revelatory, thinks Boyle, but—pace Ricoeur—not in the same way. Leaving aside the sacred literature for a later stage of his argument, he identifies the nonpurposive or disinterested character of secular literature to be "that it exploits writing in order to give pleasure, to entertain."[5] How, then, does it reveal truth? Boyle argues that it does so in two ways, one in employing the ordinary language of communication, so that not all fiction is entirely metaphorical. (Dickens's creation, Mrs. Jellyby, is not a metaphor, he says, but a type of someone we know in everyday life.) The second way is the way in which fiction lies on a spectrum of "writtenness." Pure writtenness is to be found in literature where the author is entirely absent from the text— think perhaps of the books of the Law in the Pentateuch. And pure orality is the everyday speech of one person to another, where the author is simply just there in front of you. But the more that fiction can subdue or erase authorship (and of course Boyle does not believe that this can or should ever be fully attained, disagreeing once again with Ricoeur) the more it enters into the area in which it can become revelatory of truth about life. Where fiction achieves this level of writtenness, it overlaps with Sacred Scripture, since *some* Sacred Scripture cannot entirely erase its authorship (perhaps Ecclesiastes or the Psalms might be examples of this).

The major criticisms of Boyle's argument focus on his use of two key terms, "truth" and "purpose."[6] Caery Evangelist challenges Boyle's view that the distinguishing characteristic of secular literature, especially fiction, is that it is noninstrumental writing for the sake of pleasure on the grounds that

[4] Ibid., 125.

[5] Ibid., 126.

[6] *Sacred Imagination*, ed. Charles B. Gordon and Margaret Monahan Hogan (Portland, OR: University of Portland Press, 2009).

both authors and readers would not explain literature solely as giving pleasure. Something more attracts us to it. Second, she wonders how we can talk about writing as noninstrumental and yet say that it is a vehicle for universal truth.[7] Molly Hiro[8] disagrees with the univocal notion of truth that Boyle seems to employ when he argues that "the revelation at the heart of secular literature is in the deepest sense a moral revelation, and therefore it is a revelation of God." This view leads him to say that "if we believe the teachings of the Catholic Church to be true statements about human life, then we must necessarily expect literature that is true to life to reflect and corroborate them, whether or not it is written by Catholics."[9]

Both critics have something to offer, though both can be challenged. Evangelist may be confusing purpose and consequence. So, her alternative to Boyle's view is to define literature as "imaginative invention that seeks to open the door to possibilities about what we think about, respond to, and experience in the world we inhabit."[10] Her substitution of "imaginative invention" for Boyle's weaker notion of entertainment or pleasure solves the problem that pleasure, still less entertainment, should be thought of as the only purpose of the author or reader of a fiction. The greatest works of fiction may have at best a highly refined and somewhat unusual notion of entertainment, one that can perhaps seem dangerously close to fear or horror or pathos. But the suggestion that such fiction "seeks to open the door" to something or other is a less happy choice of words, since it implies that the imaginative invention of the fiction is instrumental to some essentially moral purpose lying deeper in the authorial imagination and uncovered in the act

[7] Caery Evangelist, "Imaginative Inventions: A Purposive Account of Literature," in ibid., 67–77.

[8] Molly Hiro, "Between Truth and Truths," in ibid., 78–90.

[9] Boyle, *Sacred and Secular Scriptures*, 139, quoted in ibid., 81.

[10] Evangelist, "Imaginative Inventions," 76.

of reading. What Evangelist may be missing in Boyle's account is that he clearly thinks that the communication of truth can occur without any intention to do so. And if we ask how this happens, then we will end up talking about the imagination. So, imaginative invention by all means, but in such a way that any revelation will be an unintended consequence, not an explicit purpose. If it were the latter, it would indeed become didactic and escape the conditions of fiction.

Hiro's problem is that while she may be correct to challenge a univocal notion of truth, she is mistaken in her evident assumption that when Boyle says that the teachings of the Catholic Church are "true statements about human life," he is necessarily thinking about the surface meaning of dogmatic utterances. It would be folly to imagine that literature that is true to life must "reflect and corroborate" the bodily resurrection of Jesus or the virgin birth or the immaculate conception of Mary. But that such literature will support the Catholic understanding that the divine is present in the mundane, that grace is everywhere, and that the meaning of "God" is "love," this is not at all such a stretch. There are many truths in fiction, and most fiction is not trying to address one big Truth. But to recognize a difference between truths and Truth is not at all to say that there is a discrepancy between them. To return for a moment to the language of our earlier considerations, Truth is "the matter" behind religious and imaginative experience alike, that which is there but always just beyond our grasp, the mystery of the meaning of the whole.

Returning for a few moments to Coleridge's distinction between fancy and imagination may help us to move forward. The author is engaged at the level of the secondary imagination and utilizes fancy in the process of fashioning the work of art. The author's creativity is thus a product of fancy and (secondary) imagination, which we might restate in terms of our current discussion as the craft of writing that produces a narrative that may indeed represent truths but that is not written with

the intention of doing so (nonpurposive, then). Some works
are sufficiently wise and complex and suggestive of more that
the act of reading produces an awareness of something more
or something beyond the narrative, something that somehow
escapes articulation, something that in Boyle's words gives
rise "to a meaning that can only be elucidated by theological
exegesis." In other words, some fictions touch on the transcendent, even if they are unaware of it, and their analysis from a
theological perspective can to a degree show how that is the
case, without ever *explaining* the transcendent. And, most important, in that "theological exegesis" the work is made richer
for the reader, even and especially for the reader who is a
person of faith. Secular fiction can teach the person of faith
something about the mysterious object of that faith, though
the author of the fiction may be unaware that this is possible
and would, presumably, never be consciously intending this
kind of pedagogical purpose.

Paul Ricoeur's position deserves a little more attention than
Boyle seems willing to give to it. Boyle's critique of Ricoeur,
albeit a reverential critique, is that he is wrong to suggest that
all texts, sacred and secular alike, are revelatory in the same
way and that he is wrong to suggest that the authorial intention is *never* significant, that whatever purpose there may be
in the fiction lies in the text. While Boyle sees some overlapping
between sacred and secular along the spectrum of writtenness,
he believes that Ricoeur collapses any substantial differences
between them. For Boyle they are essentially distinct but have
some relevance to one another; for Ricoeur, they are essentially
the same. Ricoeur's perspective, however, is a little more subtle
than a simple conflation of sacred and secular.[11] In his discussion of "poetic discourse," he introduces the notion of "the
world of the text," by which he means "that what is finally to

[11] Paul Ricoeur, "Toward a Hermeneutic of the Idea of Revelation," *Harvard
Theological Review* 70, no. 1/2 (January–April 1977): 1–37.

be understood in a text is not the author or his presumed intention, nor is it the immanent structure or structures of the text, but rather the sort of world intended beyond the text as its reference." The alternatives often proposed between the authorial intention and the structure of the text itself are "vain." Instead, he proposes we consider that the text refers to its world, and "the world of the text designates the reference of the work of discourse, not what is said, but about what it is said."[12] In poetic discourse, which is non-referential and metaphorical, there truly is revelation, but Ricoeur is at some pains to be clear that scriptural and nonscriptural poetic discourse are not identical. The latter is "capable of entering into resonance" with scriptural revelation, which suggests a relationship that is not an identity. But although such revelation is nontheistic, nonreligious, and nonbiblical, it can yet be revelatory "because it incarnates a concept of truth that escapes the definition by adequation as well as the criteria of falsification and verification."

> Here truth no longer means verification, but manifestation, i.e., letting what shows itself be. What shows itself is in each instance a proposed world, a world I may inhabit and wherein I can project my ownmost possibilities. It is in this sense of manifestation that language in its poetic function is a vehicle of revelation.[13]

The most important consequence of this view is that biblical revelation does not lie so much in the text as in the world the text opens out before us, one we can "inhabit." At the same time as drawing this structural identity between poetic discourse in biblical and nonbiblical writing, Ricoeur allows that biblical revelation has a kind of autonomy. The rules of herme-

---

[12] Ibid., 23.
[13] Ibid., 25.

neutics are not different, but biblical poetic discourse is "a unique case because all its partial forms of discourse are referred to that Name which is the point of intersection and the vanishing point of all our discourse about God, the name of the unnameable." The two forms of poetic discourse in general and biblical poetic discourse in particular exhibit a "paradoxical homology." [14]

"Religious" Fiction and the World of the Text

The category of "religious fiction" is particularly elusive. Does this mean fiction that is written to promote a religious worldview or to reflect the world of some particular religious tradition? Is it perhaps fiction that is didactic or pedagogical in intent, maybe even apologetic, so that the author's hope is that the reader will somehow be enlightened to follow the right path or converted to an entirely new path? Is the term really code for "morally uplifting" stories or stories about wholly admirable, indeed holy, exemplars of human living? Or could it be that the label "religious" might be applied to works that would seem to many religious people to be anything but? To give an obvious example, Flannery O'Connor's first novel, *Wise Blood*, is about a man who preaches "the Church of Jesus Christ without Jesus Christ" in a godless town and with a set of characters who, it would seem, have nothing religious about them at all. Surrounding Hazel Motes are a "preacher" who pretends to be blind to make money under false pretenses, a developmentally challenged boy who mistakes a mummy for a religious object, a young girl out to get a man at whatever cost, a very unattractive prostitute, and a number of equally unsavory minor characters. There is very little if any goodness in these characters. They are all lost, in a way, and if salvation is present at all it resides in Hazel Motes's decision to blind

---

[14] Ibid., 26.

himself. The world of the text seems so unpromising, and yet it might be possible to name this a religious novel, if indeed the text is letting what shows itself be, as Ricoeur has it. Whatever revelation there might be here, albeit secular revelation, it is most certainly not in the text, but perhaps it is in the world of the text.

Any novelist of any faith or none must "be humble in the face of what-is," to use O'Connor's phrase,[15] without distorting it or sentimentalizing it, but if this is the case, what distinction can there be between a secular novel and a religious one? It is possible that Stephen Boyle is on to something when he talks of those "secular" works that overlap with biblical literature by disclosing "a meaning that can only be elucidated by theological exegesis," but only so long as the theological exegesis does not cannibalize the secular revelation displayed to make it serve "religious" ends. It would also need to be the case that the exegete would attend to the world of the text, as much if not more than the text itself. If you stick to the text, *Wise Blood* is bizarre, distinctly antireligious in its conclusions. But the world disclosed by the text is another matter altogether, in O'Connor's case, that life "has, for all its horror, been found by God to be worth dying for." And lest we imagine that she can simply be classified as religious, she adds that a Catholic who is a writer "will be more than ever concerned to have his work stand on its own feet and be complete and self-sufficient and impregnable in its own right."[16]

At this point we need to admit that the taxonomy is a little more complicated than we have so far seen it. There is religious fiction and there is secular fiction, if we recognize that authorial purpose has some role in its classification, and here we sympathize with Boyle more than with Ricoeur. But, this does

---

[15] "The Church and the Fiction Writer," in *Flannery O'Connor: Collected Works*, 808.

[16] Ibid.

not mean that all fiction intended to be religious in some way can be considered revelatory, or that all fiction intended to be secular is thereby disqualified from being revelatory. Moreover, which fiction is revelatory and which is not cannot in the end be a function of authorial purpose, and here we side with Ricoeur. It cannot then be a matter of assigning revelatory significance to fiction that is somehow religious and excluding all secular fiction. Serious fiction, ostensibly religious in some discernible way or determinedly secular in its worldview, always displays a surplus of meaning that was not and is not controlled by the author and that is not entirely accessible to the reader. The text opens out a world, in Ricoeur's language, or—in ours—it is in "the space between" the reader and the text that imaginative possibility arises and the aesthetic object is created. Fiction that is simply didactic or sentimental, which is the weakness of much "religious" fiction, or fiction that exists simply to entertain, however skillfully it does this, which is a kind of fiction that can never be classified as in any sense religious or open to theological exegesis, simply does not display a world beyond the text. It is what it is. At the same time, we need to recognize that authorial purpose may not have the last word here either, since some fiction that sets out simply to entertain can at times escape that limited objective and achieve some revelatory status. One sees something of this kind of development whenever, for example, a writer of crime fiction or spy stories is said to have "transcended the genre."

The conclusion to be drawn from these distinctions is that the term "religious fiction" is not helpful in identifying which writing is serious or even revelatory. To be serious or revelatory requires that, however ostensibly religious or secular a novel might be, there is a world of the text that lies beyond the text in which imagination can play. For fiction to be classified as religious, it does not have to be about a saint or by a saint (another opinion rebuffed by O'Connor), but it does have to open out into a world in which the claim of faith is admissible.

So does secular fiction, if it is to rise to being revelatory. Ricoeur
had something like this in mind when he cautioned against a
potential impasse between biblical revelation and philosophy.
"If the unacceptable pretentious claim of the idea of revelation,"
he wrote, "is in the final analysis that of a *sacrificium intellectus*
and of a total heteronomy under the verdict of the magisterium, the opposed pretentious claim of philosophy is the claim
to a complete transparency of truth and a total autonomy of
the thinking subject." The claim of revelation must be "an ap-
peal which does not force one to accept its message,"[17] while
philosophy must avoid thinking of rationalism as the only
show in town that deals in truth. Transposing this distinction
to the relationship between faith and fiction, one can reasonably argue that all fiction that is in any sense revelatory will
leave the reader free to create the aesthetic object by entering
into the world of the text that lies beyond the actual text itself.
The religious fiction against which O'Connor so wittily and
forcefully inveighed in her few published essays is exactly the
kind of writing that sets out to enforce its religious claim. It
presents religious "truth" as if it is self-evident, and the great
American Catholic public with whom O'Connor had to deal
often could not stomach *her* fiction because it wasn't "uplifting" or wasn't either by a saint or about a saint. In parallel
fashion, secular fiction that we are not considering here is
either bad fiction which, like bad religious fiction, sets out to
enforce a claim on our attention, or it is fiction that may be
perfectly good of its kind but has no purpose other than to
entertain. Once again, Boyle's insistence that all fiction is un-
purposed (mostly true) and only exists to entertain (too strong
a claim, making fiction out to be too weak a vehicle of truth,
however indistinctly intended by its authors) seems like an
oversimplification.

[17] Ricoeur, "Toward a Hermeneutic," 19.

To clarify these interrelationships, it will be helpful to turn back briefly to the distinctions we made in the earlier chapters between faith and knowledge, on the one hand, and between faith and "religion," on the other. The entire scholastic and neo-scholastic consideration of so-called natural religion, that is, the knowledge of God that we can ascertain through the use of human reason, is quite helpful. There are considerable differences among these philosophers and theologians over the possibility of natural knowledge of God, but even those who think some knowledge is possible, Aquinas, for example, are insistent that it is extremely limited knowledge and, more important, that this knowledge does not produce faith. Natural knowledge of God can support faith—"faith seeking understanding"—but it cannot bring it about. In more recent times, most clearly in the writings of Pierre Rousselot, we saw a sophisticated interweaving of natural knowledge and faith. We cannot have faith in something that has no intellectual component, but the credibility of an object of faith does not produce faith. On the question of the relationship between faith and religion in general, we have to turn back to Bonhoeffer, who argued that in our modern world we need to uncouple faith in the crucified Christ from "religion" and instead understand any living with and within the suffering of humanity as genuine discipleship of Christ without the necessity of any thematized relationship to Christianity, or any other religious tradition for that matter.

Following Rousselot and Bonhoeffer on the two issues of the faith/knowledge relationship and the discipleship/religion relationship enables us to see, for the sake of example, how we can classify much so-called Christian fiction as unrevelatory and simply not serious, in religious or secular terms, and a novel like *Wise Blood* as a deeply revelatory text that falls into the overlap that Boyle sees between biblical and secular revelation but whose "revelation," following Ricoeur, can be encountered only by entering the world of the text and not by plumbing authorial purpose. "Christian fiction," an Amazon book category, is distinguished by being openly religious, sometimes ostentatiously Christian, and at other times wildly erratic but passing itself off as compatible with Christianity. Much but by no means all of it is badly written, it sells very well and is often extravagantly praised by its delighted readers. *Wise Blood* is on the surface a disturbingly antireligious work, never a best seller but also never out of print in the half-century since it was first published.

Christian fiction is a large and varied category of writings. One example of the worst kind, admittedly an easy target, is *Angels Walking*, a novel by the best-selling author Karen Kingsbury.[18] This and the other novels in the Angels Walking series explore the adventures of a band of angels led by the somewhat improbably named Orlon.[19] In the opening pages of this, the first in the series, Orlon explains to his band of angels that they have to go off and try to save the souls of a washed-up baseball player and his former girlfriend, to encourage them because if they fail to recover, or if the angels fail in their task, then a child who is to be born to save humankind will never be born. And by the way, his name, equally improbably, is Dallas Garner. At the time of writing these words Amazon listed over 1,200 reviews of the book with an average rating of five stars. But not all Christian fiction is so easily dismissible. William Paul Young's *The Shack*[20] is still a major best seller after five years and, though its theology is a little weird and its apologetic purpose fairly evident, there is a measure of ambiguity and challenge in the text that saves it from the merely didactic. At what some would consider to be a more elevated level, the

[18] Karen Kingsbury, *Angels Walking* (Nashville, TN: Howard Books, 2015).
[19] Orlon was an early synthetic fiber, a forerunner of polyester, which may or may not be relevant.
[20] William Paul Young, *The Shack* (Newbury Park, CA: Windblown Media, 2007).

science-fiction writing of C. S. Lewis is quite skillful but never rises above the effort to persuade. Lewis himself was not given to considering there might be two sides to any religious question, and the novels suffer from this.

Rather than drawing distinctions between religious and secular fiction or light reading and serious fiction, we will be on firmer ground by sticking with the category of revelatory fiction, but interpreting the word "revelatory" to include openness to a faith perspective. Just as the word revelatory has no necessary connection to biblical or distinctly Christian revelation, so the word "faith" is not tied to faith in some particular tradition, or faith in Jesus Christ, or even to religious faith at all. At the heart of the struggle to believe, religious or secular, is a willingness to be open to the possibility of transcendence. When we encounter a fiction that opens to us a world of possibility, the world of the text, the act of reading once again recalls the act of faith. Each is an imaginative appropriation of something beyond the self, distinctly personal but at the same time evoked by a response to something quite other than the self, something we find in the world of the text.

The "Catholic Novel": What Is to Be Done?

A number of distinguished writers, principal among them Paul Elie[21] and Dana Gioia,[22] have drawn attention in the last couple of years to what they consider to be the near-disappearance either of novels that take questions of faith seriously (Elie) or of novels through which the Catholic religious and intellectual tradition continues to be present and respected

[21] Paul Elie, "Has Fiction Lost Its Faith?," *New York Times* (December 19, 2012).
[22] Dana Gioia, "The Catholic Writer Today," *First Things* (December 2013); available online at http://www.firstthings.com/article/2013/12/the-catholic -writer-today.

in the pluralistic conversation of American literary culture (Gioia). They are puzzled. If Catholics comprise about a quarter of the American public, they ask, why are they not more prominent in the literary arts? Once upon a time they were, and they were respected for it, according to Gioia. Now the topic of religious faith or the lack of it is largely ignored or ridiculed, in Elie's view. Though it is not their central concern, both authors in their different ways imply that the health of the novel cannot be separated from much deeper questions about the place of religious faith in American life, indeed in American Catholic life. So what happens if we put the concerns of Elie and Gioia into a larger frame of reference?

The disappearance of the Catholic novel in the sense in which at least Elie and Gioia seem to mean it should be a surprise to no one and in fact may not be a matter for much concern. In fact, a healthier situation is envisaged in a number of books that Elie and Gioia seem not to know, or at least don't consider relevant to their respective Jeremiads. Nicholas Ripatrazone's 2013 book[23] has chapters examining in detail the work of Ron Hansen, André Dubus, and Paul Mariani, and the final two chapters consider a whole list of less well-known authors writing serious Catholic novels and poetry at the present day (perhaps Ripatrazone's work could encourage a reframing of the question that so concerns Elie and Gioia, namely, that we should be asking not why Catholic novels or novels of faith are not appearing, but why Catholics aren't reading those that are definitely available). But his first chapter is perhaps the most significant, analyzing works by Jeffrey Eugenides and Don DeLillo. Here he explores what he calls "the Catholic literary paradox," namely, that there is no clarity about who is or is not a Catholic writer, that lapsed or ex-Catholics might be included (or not), even if they reject the

---

[23] Nicholas Ripatrazone, *The Fine Delight: Postconciliar Catholic Literature* (Eugene, OR: Cascade Books, 2013).

label (as Graham Greene famously did, but to no avail), and that cultural forces inside and outside the church have had an impact.

Several other texts take up similar arguments to those of Ripatrazone. There is Anita Gandolfo's somewhat older book, *Testing the Faith: The New Catholic Fiction in America*[24] and the much more recent work of John C. Waldmeir, *Cathedrals of Bone: The Role of the Body in Contemporary Catholic Literature*.[25] They all three in their different ways make the point that something changed in the way Catholics understand faith in the aftermath of Vatican II and that this illumines a lot of subsequent Catholic fiction. The Catholic novel that is not going merely to be an exercise in religious nostalgia will have to reflect the Catholicism of today, warts and all. If we start, as Gioia seems to, with the assumption that the church is at the very least going to purgatory in a handbasket, then presumably we should be looking for literature that explores this decline and not novels that hark back to a golden age, however much we might want that still to be the case. Ripatrazone and Waldmeier in particular seem to be approaching the topic in a much more fruitful way than Elie and Gioia by homing in on what Catholic fiction is like today, rather than starting from why there is so little. In light of the many authors whom they discuss at length (including Mary Gordon, a curious omission from both Elie and Gioia's essays), simple regret for the passing of Catholic novels or novels of faith may seem distinctly premature, if not even a little foolish.

There is no doubt that the "Catholic culture" that existed in the United States and much of western Europe through the middle of the twentieth century is gone for good, and that fact

---

[24] Anita Gandolfo, *Testing the Faith: The New Catholic Fiction in America* (Westport, CT: Praeger, 1992).

[25] John C. Waldmeir, *Cathedrals of Bone: The Role of the Body in Contemporary Catholic Literature* (New York: Fordham University Press, 2009).

alone goes a long way toward explaining the demise of its particular literary counterpart. Looking forward, however, there are at least three aspects of emerging Catholicism that need to be taken into account in determining the fate of the Catholic novel. The first takes up the demise of Catholic culture and reflects on what Staf Hellemans has called the emergence of Catholicism as a "religionized" religion.[26] The second looks to the implications of the theology of grace developed at Vatican II, especially in the Decree on the Church, *Lumen Gentium*. And the third, taking inspiration from that other great conciliar document, *Gaudium et Spes*, the Pastoral Constitution on the Church in the World of Today, addresses the contemporary phenomenon of Catholicism as a church coexisting in dialogue with other religions and even with the secular world. If these three phenomena are truly components of today's Catholicism, what does this mean for what a "Catholic" novel would look like?

The preeminent cultural phenomenon affecting American Catholicism today is what Ripatrazone identifies as the divorce between faith and religion, or what William V. D'Antonio and his team describe in *American Catholics in Transition*[27] as the separation between identity and commitment. Using their demographic insights it is not hard to see that "Catholic culture" is much more complicated than it once was. It is no longer monolithic; it shows the Catholic public's profile to be very similar in many respects to that of Americans in general, particularly in the insistence on personal autonomy in ethical decision making. Moreover, today's Catholics demonstrate an ongoing identification with the Catholic tradition but a waning

[26] Staf Hellemans, "Tracking the New Shape of the Catholic Church in the West," in *Towards a New Catholic Church in Advanced Modernity: Transformations, Visions, Tensions*, ed. Staf Hellemans and Jozef Wissink, Tilburg Theological Studies 5 (Zurich and Berlin: Lit, 2012), 19–50.

[27] William V. D'Antonio, Michele Dillon, and Mary L. Gautier, *American Catholics in Transition* (Lanham, MD: Rowman & Littlefield, 2013).

level of participation in worship and sharply declining Catholic literacy. This naturally leads to some inconsistencies; for example, a far larger percentage of self-described Catholics think the sacraments are very important than actually participate in them on any regular basis. As one might expect, the youngest generation of adults, the so-called millennials, are sharply distinct from older groups in their level of participation. More surprising and perhaps more disconcerting, women seem to have overtaken men on many of the issues of dissatisfaction with the institutional church. But what D'Antonio has convincingly demonstrated is that across the generations, genders, and levels of religious practice, Catholic people continue to have a sense for what is central to their faith. In large numbers they show awareness that the most important elements are belief in the bodily resurrection of Jesus, in the role of the sacraments, in devotion to the Virgin Mary, and in concern to aid the poor. As Jim Davidson, the Purdue University sociologist of religion and a one-time member of the team that produced earlier versions of this survey, once remarked in a conversation at Fairfield University, if this is what people believe, what are the bishops so worried about?

If, as Paul Elie claims, what are lacking are novels that examine the question of faith in the context of our world, not that of even the relatively recent past, then the cultural shape of the Catholic world will have to appear in literature in a fragmented manner, to be true to the reality. Priestly authority is no longer taken for granted, any more than regular worship is an indicator of a "good Catholic," and the lives of today's Catholics are indistinguishable in most respects from those of Americans of other religious traditions and none. This would seem to enforce a kind of interiority on the contemporary dilemmas of belief and unbelief. Ours is a much less social world than it once was, whether we are talking about the village, the neighborhood, or the parish. Indeed, for contemporary Catholics it is often the case that the remains of the culture are less a support to faith than they are a challenge. While the affective support of a living community has waned considerably, clericalism and its attendant lay subservience have evidently had greater staying power. At the same time, turning back to the Catholic novels of the preconciliar era it is hard not to be influenced by the knowledge we have now, that perhaps we did not have then, that there is a shadow side to Catholic culture as it was and to its clerical dimension in particular.

This question of Catholic culture is complicated by the movement of Catholicism toward becoming a religionized religion or "a church that has been reduced to the core business of religion," in Staf Hellemans's words. The most important consequence of the dismantling of the Catholic subculture of preconciliar times is that today the connections that Catholics make between their religious faith and practice, on the one hand, and their daily lives, on the other, are negotiated as individuals. There is no such thing anymore as "the way Catholics vote" or, perhaps, the choices they make about the books and journals they read or the Netflix shows they favor. When the institutional church campaigns for religious freedom or against the "evil" of health insurance covering contraceptives, its failure to carry most Catholics along with it illustrates this phenomenon of religionization. While practicing Catholics (an unsteady category today) obviously continue to find eucharistic worship to be spiritually fulfilling, they overwhelmingly pay little or no attention to church teaching, however authoritative, that does not conform to their personal convictions. Whether this is a refreshing sign of Christian adulthood or the deplorable evidence of declining faithfulness, it does create a quandary for the Catholic novelist. When religious practice and daily life have little explicit connection to one another, where is the faith that Elie's novelist ought to be concerned with? And if Catholicism has become religionized, how can Gioia's novelists speak out and reflect a Catholic culture that has evaporated?

This apparently gloomy assessment can be modified by attention to the second and third aspects of postconciliar Catholicism, a richer theology of grace, and a humbler relationship to the wisdom of other traditions and of the secular world. While there are a number of plausible candidates for the title of "principal theme at Vatican II," the idea of "grace" certainly has to be a favorite. While the theological complexities of grace, still more the Byzantine structure of medieval ruminations about grace, are often confusing in the extreme, at heart the term "grace" simply refers to the loving presence of God. The complexity comes from the academician's lust to count the ways. Moreover, it is because *Lumen Gentium* takes the grace of God to be universally available that *Gaudium et Spes* can conclude that there is theological wisdom in the signs of the times and that the secular world may have much to teach the church.

Once we break loose from the conviction that somehow the Catholic tradition has privileged access to God's grace, then novels of faith written by Catholics will have no need to concern themselves with Catholicism at all, though of course they may choose to do so. Their objective surely has to be to explore the gracious presence of God, and the sinfulness that is its shadow side, in ways that evince the continuity of what we have to call "a Catholic way of looking at things." But here Ron Hansen has warned us that " 'Catholic Fiction' is a slippery category and "probably more functional in the classroom than it is in criticism." He made this comment in an interview immediately after declaring that "what perhaps finally distinguishes a Catholic fiction writer from all others is the Yes—And rather than the Yes—But approach to their subjects." But, he asked, "doesn't that fit the fiction of Eudora Welty and Saul Bellow?"[28] Here we see a good illustration of the "Catholic

[28] See http://dappledthings.org/2101/a-novel-vocation-a-conversation -with-ron-hansen/.

literary paradox" that is at the heart of Nicholas Ripatrazone's book. While Hansen is on good theological ground in identifying "yes—and" as distinctive of the Catholic analogical approach to life, it is not the case that only Catholics approach life this way. Anyone who thinks that human beings and human society are better understood as a complex mix of good and evil or sin and grace, and not divided between good and evil or sin and grace, belongs to this "Catholic" camp. If you remember the old Alaska-based TV show *Northern Exposure*, or you have been lucky enough to read about the sinful saints in Gloria Naylor's *Bailey's Café*,[29] or can't wait for the next volume in Louise Penny's detective fiction set in the little Quebec village of Three Pines, you will know exactly what this means.[30] As Georges Bernanos famously ended his *Diary of a Country Priest*, "Grace is everywhere."

What is sometimes hard to keep in mind is that a serious writer who is a Catholic is not going to set out to write anything other than the best novel of which he or she is at that time capable. It is conceivable that its location or its characters, or some of them, might be Catholics. They equally well might not, and neither choice makes it more rather than less likely that the result will be a Catholic novel. If it turns out to be a Catholic novel, it will be because of a particular sensibility that informs whatever the story is about. The sensibility cannot dictate what the story is about, still less how it will work itself out. But if it is clearly present then it doesn't matter if the topic is Joan of Arc or Joseph Stalin, or the context is a beach vacation or an abortion clinic.

For all her very traditional Catholicism, Flannery O'Connor seems to have anticipated Vatican II's teaching on grace when she wrote that the Catholic writer "will feel life from the standpoint of the central Christian mystery: that it has, for all its

---

[29] Gloria Naylor, *Bailey's Café* (New York: Harcourt Brace Jovanovich, 1992).
[30] Chap. 8 will consider these texts in detail.

horror, been found by God to be worth dying for." Just so Georges Bernanos, an even more conservative Catholic, with his remark that "grace is everywhere." Thanking God for dappled things is all very well, but finding the love of God in the world of Hazel Motes is a far greater challenge. "Life" and "everywhere" are not words that limit grace to Christians, let alone to the Catholic world.

Is it then the case that the whole notion of a Catholic novel is in fact a false category? There are books by Catholics, books about Catholic people or Catholic culture, books that explore the history, good and bad, of the Catholic tradition. But as Ripatrazone so clearly pointed out, it is very hard to pin down what constitutes a Catholic book. "You'll know it when you see it" is perhaps a cheap way out of the quandary, except that it suggests that a Catholic book might simply be a book that challenges and/or enriches the Catholic sensibility of the reader. Jews and Baptists don't care if a book is a Catholic novel, just if it is a good one, and this may be the healthier attitude. But if the reader is a Catholic in any of the ways that we could list (practicing, ex, recovering, questioning, excommunicated, divorced and remarried, and so on) then that reader's Catholicism will be a feature in the process of determining the aesthetic object. Once we have limited the significance of the authorial purpose and distinguished the text from the world that the text opens out, then the explicit Catholicism of the author or of the text is of much less significance than we might previously have thought.

While it is reassuring to know that there are many "Catholic" authors out there still, and many more who address Catholic themes in some way, it is more instructive to consider the ways in which secular novels address and even nourish the religious imagination. Once we established the symmetry between the act of faith and the act of reading, and identified a distinct affinity between the matter of fiction and the mysterious object of faith, it was only a matter of time before we could conclude,

like so many others before us, that all serious fiction is susceptible of theological exegesis, to use Ricoeur's formulation. It
remains in the third and final part of this book to flesh out this
assertion by examining the value to the religious imagination
of some examples of serious fiction, bearing in mind that what
makes them theologically significant is not the presence of
religious themes in the texts, still less the preferences of their
creators, but that they are susceptible in the space between to
participation in the creation of aesthetic objects that engage
transcendence. In doing this, we will achieve two further ob-
jectives. We will see how fiction can help stimulate the religious
imagination in an age when its decline is directly connected
to the declining vitality of religious practice. And we will be
able to formulate a modest effort at a theology of fiction. When
we ask what fiction is doing, we will find the answer to be
surprisingly close to the answer to that other question: what
is the point of faith?

Part Three

The Wounded Angel

■ ■ ■ ■ ■ ■　*Chapter Seven*　■ ■ ■ ■ ■ ■

The Sacred and the Secular

Looking

It may seem quite strange that in a book that is largely focused on literature we should begin this third and final section with an examination of the importance of looking. And yet the kind of attention that is required in sustained looking at an art object is remarkably similar to the kind of attention required in reading a serious work of literature. What is reading, after all, if not a process of sustained attention to an object that in a way is questioning us and inviting our response? Somehow or other, "what is going on here?" is always in the back of the mind of the observer of art and the reader of fiction. Some art and some fiction may invite the response, "Not much!" and although this does not invalidate the beauty of the painting or the quality of the writing, neither will it detain us beyond decoration or entertainment. In the case of art and fiction that cannot be classified this way, it elicits the question from the viewer or reader, "Yes, but what is *really* going on here?" Recalling Wolfgang Iser's helpful distinction, the first kind of work is one to which we respond with an attitude. We classify it and assign it a place that requires and stimulates no further thought. But the second kind of work is one that we are drawn to interpret. That is, we suspect there is a meaning in the work that our attentiveness may lead to our discovering, however imperfectly, to our benefit. The work of art, painting, or novel

155

is not changed in any way by this decision to look deeper. We indeed may be changed by the encounter with this work of art, but the change that may occur in us will do so in the way we create the aesthetic object in the space between our individual concrete subjectivity and the equally concrete text or painting. In accepting the claim that it is making on us, we recognize at once the surplus of meaning that makes such a claim possible and the responsibility we have to recognize its integrity and our own. The ethics of appreciation require disciplined looking and hearing, which allow the work to exercise its influence, coupled with open and honest awareness of our own response to the claim. All of this is worked out in the space between the interpreting subject and the objective text. The objectivity of the text limits the range of authentic interpretations, but the individuality of the interpreter means that no two interpretations need be or are likely to be exactly the same. Conversation between different interpretations is only possible when both honor the integrity of the text.

Aside from the setting, which is a well-known spot to Finns, everything else in Hugo Simberg's picture of *The Wounded Angel* invites questions. Why are two young boys transporting the angel? Is the angel a he or a she or, more theologically sophisticated, neither, being pure spirit? What has happened to the angel? One wing is damaged, suggesting a fall from the sky, like Icarus, but the hurt may have occurred some other less accidental way. Which? Why is the angel clasping a small bunch of white flowers in one hand, flowers that are also blooming on the ground? Then there is the white bandanna around the angel's head. Is the angel suffering from a head wound, or perhaps blindfolded? Turning our attention to the two boys, we see that they grasp the poles of the stretcher quite effortlessly, because angels are after all presumably weightless. The boy in front, dressed all in black, tramps doggedly along, staring ahead, a serious expression on his face. What is he thinking? Or is he just focused on getting there? And where is the "there" toward which they are heading? Is there medical care suitable for angels somewhere in the neighborhood? The boy who is bringing up the rear is decidedly more enigmatic. He is paying more attention to us than to the path ahead. When we see the picture for the first time it is probable that it is *his* gaze to which *our* gaze gravitates. He is the one who draws us into the picture. His gaze is in some way the conduit of the claim the picture makes on us. But what is he thinking? He is looking serious, of course, but is it not the case that there is also something accusing in his look? Is it entirely fanciful to see him effectively saying something like "why did you do this?" or even "this is your fault!"? There is really no doubt that the way in which he is looking out at the one viewing the painting demands reaction and response.

One way to see this painting is as a statement about the relationship between the secular and the sacred. The two boys represent the everyday world at its helpful best. There is someone in need? Then we must meet that need, however odd or unusual the needy one turns out to be. Carrying an angel on a stretcher is certainly not an everyday activity, but it is being conducted in a very matter-of-fact way. The angel, in contrast, can represent not only something spiritual or holy or unworldly but also the fragility that goes with it. The boys are sturdy, robust, and rooted to the earth. The angel is weightless, almost floating above the stretcher, yet somehow hurt if not permanently damaged. How the relationship between earth and heaven is asserted is, however, not in the figures in the painting itself but in the work of interpretation that we, the viewers, bring to it. Some may want to see the picture as an image of the interdependence of the secular and the sacred, while others might prefer to see it as a warning about the damage we can do to the sense of the sacred and the way in which innocents (the boys) can teach us a lesson about how to heal the injury we have inflicted. And perhaps still others will see the painting confirming the parlous condition of anything spiritual in today's godless world, for the boys are surely more vigorous than the angel. The components of the painting and the psyche of the individual interpreters will lead to one of these or of doubtless many other possible solutions to "the meaning of the painting." Or may, indeed, leave some interpreters deliberately not deciding for one meaning or another. Surplus of meaning can lead to different interpretations or to luxuriating in the plethora of possibilities and leaving it at that.

One way of seeing the painting is as a commentary on the connections between the act of faith and the act of reading. And so it is. We can see this painting as a commentary on the act of faith, and we can see it as a statement about imaginative attentiveness to a work of art. One need not see it in either way, of course, since the surplus of meaning that a work of art exhibits allows for potentially endless variations in interpretation. But any interpretation beyond the naïve realism of "it's just a picture of two boys carrying an angel who crash-landed" or "Kirsti fell off the ladder at the school's Christmas pageant and is being rushed to hospital" recognizes the open-endedness of possibilities, and this itself says something about both the act of faith and the act of reading.

Viewed as a commentary on the act of faith, *The Wounded Angel* puts in the foreground two modern challenges: faith is always in tension with doubt; and the secular and the sacred have an unusual relationship to one another, if they are viewed from an earthly vantage point. The issue of faith and doubt leads us to focus on the figure of the angel. We could imagine that the angel itself suffered from doubt and fell to earth, like Peter failing to walk on water because of his lack of faith. But we might be on firmer ground if we think of the wounded angel as a commentary on the fragility of the religious imagination. Angels are representatives of a traditional vision of heaven, whence they go about their business as messengers or couriers between God and the world. Faith in God today is most commonly not connected to belief in spiritual beings like angels (which is not to say that this belief has entirely disappeared). Nevertheless, the wounded angel serves very well as an image of what happens to spiritual beings when those to whom they are directed falter in their belief in angelic reality. When the imagination can no longer assent to them, they fall to earth. And then we notice that succor for the wounded is provided by children, by those who perhaps still find it easier to believe. Looked at this way, the stare of the second boy accuses us of the crime of lack of imagination. He looks at us as a smaller child might have done when we finally explain Santa Claus, except that *he* knows we are wrong because he is indeed helping his friend to carry a real angel in real need. Something in his stare is challenging us to believe again.

If we focus a little more on the painting as a statement about the relationship between the sacred and the secular, then we may see the angel more as a figure of the weakness of contemporary faith, and the picture as a whole commending to us the need for a closer relationship between the things of the spirit and earthly reality. The angel in this picture is truly dependent on the help of human beings and connected to them through the two poles of the stretcher. There is also the small posy of flowers, perhaps given by one of the boys to lighten the atmosphere and distract the sufferer from the pain and discomfort. And, contrary to many descriptions of this painting, the angel is not blindfolded but looking down under the head-bandage at the earth beneath the stretcher. Pressing a little harder, we can also think of the angel as a messenger sent this time to alert people of faith to their need to carry and be responsible for faith in the everyday world. Bonhoeffer, it would seem, would be especially favorable to this interpretation. Two boys carrying a wounded angel nicely contrast with the *deus ex machina* who arrives from heaven to settle every issue.

Looked at from either side of the question, the painting stimulates the viewer to recognize that while faith has an intellectual component, embracing the meaning of the whole requires us to surrender to the ambiguity, or, better, to the surplus, of meaning laid out before us. The act of faith is an act of the will, informed to some degree by the reason, through which the holy itself draws us into a loving embrace whose reality can never be rationally explained. This is why in the end the various efforts at interpretation we have just considered pale into insignificance beside the quiet contemplation of this extraordinary work of art. We can certainly reap benefits from asking "what is this painting about?" and pursuing these kinds of reflections, but we are still left with the question that escapes rational response: "Yes, but what is it *really* about?" There is a mystery here that Simberg himself could not control, the "matter" that escapes full comprehension.

Turning our attention to the question of creativity in general and literary creativity in particular, we can immediately see the similarity between the act of faith and the act of seeing/ reading, since this picture invites us to interpret it in religious terms, loosely understood. The potentially religious content of our response to Simberg's painting is, however, irrelevant to the tectonics of its imaginative appropriation. We do essentially the same with any text that invites the suspicion that there is more to it than meets the eye and, indeed, that unearthing what it is about beneath the surface cannot exhaust its meaning and leaves us unable finally to answer the question, "what is it really about?" Put differently, focusing on our conviction that the meaning of any serious work of art escapes full comprehension—like the act of faith—leads inexorably to Simone Weil's view, quoted earlier, that "all art of the highest order is religious in essence," since it is a foray into the unknowable depths of transcendence, of that which goes beyond what we can ever fully know. As Martin Scorsese so eloquently put it, "Every truly great work of art orients you to what isn't there, what can't be seen or described or named."[1]

---

[1] Martin Scorsese, "Afterword," in *Approaching* Silence: *New Perspectives on Shusaku Endo's Classic Novel*, ed. Mark W. Dennis and Darren J. N. Middleton (New York: Bloomsbury, 2015), 397.

While we have drawn so many parallels between the act of faith and the act of reading, they are not the same, and their difference is instructive. There is structural similarity between the two acts. Moreover, in the way in which literature toys with the transcendent, we can grant some justice to Weil's claim that all art is "religious in essence." But at the same time we need to see that the ways in which faith and literature approach the transcendent are quite distinct. Faith, even if it is shadowed in some way by doubt, exists in the mode of commitment. While it can undoubtedly be lost, while it can grow stronger or weaker in time, if it is faith, then it is a loving relationship to the power of the holy disclosed somehow to the believer. Literature is propaedeutic to faith, in that it throws up innumerable possibilities of access to transcendence. Literature, one might say, warms up the human capacity for faith, but it does not cause it, still less does it command it. At the same time, however, literature has another equally important role. While it serves to assist the more secular mind to contemplate deeper possibilities, it can nourish the person of faith in one very important respect, broadening the range of vision so that a narrowly religious vision is exchanged for openness to the ubiquity of divine grace. When this happens, we are encountering the novel as a theological resource. Or as Ricoeur might prefer to have it, as revelatory, and potentially equally so, whether the ostensible subject is "secular" or "religious."

There are countless works of fiction to which one could turn in order to justify the claim that they both broaden the range of vision of the religious mind and open up the secular mind to hints of the transcendent. In the remainder of this chapter we will look quite closely at two such books. The first, *The Big Seven*, is a fairly recent novel by Jim Harrison, and the second, the much better known but more disturbing work of the young Flannery O'Connor, *Wise Blood*. Harrison's book, like the man himself, is a challenging blend of the raunchy and the sublime, while Flannery O'Connor's first novel digs deep into the psyches of some very sick people but succeeds in drawing out something worthy of our deepest contemplation. In both we see sin all too evidently, but grace keeps nudging its way in. One could say that both show how the Holy Spirit won't take no for an answer.

Jim Harrison's **The Big Seven**

Jim Harrison was a great American poet and a man who also wrote novels, though he has primarily been credited with the revival of the novella form, which his publisher once told him "nobody reads." He is probably best known for the novella *Legends of the Fall*, not least because it became a successful movie starring Brad Pitt and Anthony Hopkins. Most of his twenty or so works of fiction are either located in the Upper Peninsula of Michigan or feature a central character who hails from there and periodically wishes he were back, either on the farm or, even better, fishing for trout. "He" because most of Harrison's novels are written from the male point of view, most commonly a first-person narrator. The one major exception to this is *Dalva*, whose midlife female protagonist heads home to Nebraska from California, seeking as so many of Harrison's characters do to find the life they so regret having left behind. Nostalgia, solitude, and mortality are never far from the pages of these books.

But Harrison's books are also raunchy, dealing with characters and situations that are often highly politically incorrect, frequently scabrous, occasionally obscene, and almost always very, very funny. In *The Great Leader* he introduces us to the recently retired Detective Sunderson, on the trail of a very dubious leader of an equally suspect religious cult. The hunt is long and arduous and ends disastrously with a shoot-out in which Sunderson is wounded. Like many of Harrison's other books, there is a lot of alcohol and a great deal of lusting after women of various ages, many much younger than Sunderson, and almost all of whom seem unrealistically ready to oblige.

How much of this shattered life is a product of regret for his failed marriage, lost because of his alcoholism, it is not easy to tell, but some of it surely, since Sunderson is also well-read and extraordinarily thoughtful, given to deep reflection on life.

Simon Sunderson reemerges as the central character in the 2015 novel, *The Big Seven*, subtitled *A Faux Mystery*. This mystery which is not a real mystery does in fact have a mystery running through it. Who is killing off the members of the Ames clan, a band of backcountry outlaws in the Upper Peninsula of Michigan, who are a law unto themselves, who have probably killed at least one federal investigator, who treat their women abominably and subject their young females to criminal sexual activity? The hunch is that they are killing off one another, and this would certainly be no bad thing. But into this picture comes Sunderson, who inexplicably decides to spend some money he acquired by blackmailing a serial molester on a small cabin on land adjacent to that of the Ames'. The retired detective is drawn into the drama first by the murder of his young cook and housemaid killed before he can even get to know her and then by hiring her grieving sister Monica the very next day. The nineteen-year-old Monica is a great cook and an eager sex partner to the sixty-five-year-old. Sunderson sets out to help Monica and an even younger girl, whose sexual advances he thankfully rejects, to get away from the clan, and the story unfolds from there, with further shootings, poisonings, and a hanging or two. The back story continues as in the previous novel to be the one great love of his life, his ex-wife Diane. Their *rapprochement* is limited, but real. A kind of happiness, even romance, seems possible. And there is also a sort of resolution in the final pages with Sunderson's realization that he was "quite tired of being as ridiculous as a twelve-year-old boy, an aimless prisoner of sex." He has even given up whiskey for wine.

The first suspicions of a perceptive reader that there is more to this novel than the deeply disedifying storyline will probably be occasioned by the dawning awareness that "the big seven" of the title refers to the seven deadly sins of the Christian tradition. It is not long before Sunderson makes explicit reference to them and to two plans he has: one to try to do better in avoiding the sins, one to write an account of an eighth deadly sin, which he believes is violence. There are some wonderful pages in which he frankly assesses how his conduct measures up. He gives himself pretty good grades on greed and gluttony and a passing grade on anger, envy, and laziness. Pride bothers him, the pride of a divorced man who knows that he deserved it, and lechery provokes the sternest self-critique. Which it certainly should. He examines his conscience on his voyeurism, having spent too much time peeking at his teenage neighbor doing nude yoga in the open air (really?) and once, after he and Diane had adopted her, having sex with her in a hotel in Paris. This, he knows, was "a very wrong thing," but he is much more conflicted about Monica. She is too young for him at nineteen, but willing: "Her butt is beautiful but is that an excuse?" He concludes that he is being too easy on himself and that "the very idea of sex on occasion fills me with unrest and torpor as if I want it to end." But it doesn't seem to stop him.

We would probably end up deciding that Sunderson is a sad old man who ought to know better and who in the end has perhaps realized that it is time to do better were it not for two further levels of the narrative. One is the depth of reflections on a whole range of things that he treats us to in the course of telling his story. The other is his love of the outdoors in general, and of fishing in particular, both of which clearly bring the best out of him. During a fishing trip with his best buddy Marion early in the novel, he reflects as he rests from a strenuous hike that "in literature our lives were rivers," and this doesn't seem right to him. Better to think of them as creeks or rivulets, hopefully strong creeks but "you could muddy it up with carelessness." He admits to himself that he is not interested in too much change but sadly adds that he wishes he didn't end up every evening drunk and teary, thinking about the wife he had lost. A little later in the story, "Death was in his thoughts as he rested up." He thinks he would prefer a ride through the galaxies rather than heaven, which sounds boring, and, wondering if he will see Diane in the afterlife, he drifts into reflections on birds, which he had read were thought in the Middle Ages not to be present in hell. This leads him into further ruminations about Mormons and marriage in the afterlife and how there could be no divorce in heaven. And he ends by deciding he has no talent for theology.

Sunderson is not a theologian with a whole list of answers to questions that someone or other might ask, like whether there is divorce in heaven, birds in hell, or how many angels might stand on the head of a pin, but he is perhaps a better theologian than he realizes. If we think of a theologian as someone who constantly visits and revisits the time-honored questions about the limits and meaning of human life without ever producing definitive answers, then Sunderson might well be in that company. His ex-wife certainly recognizes his burgeoning interest in theological questions and gives him a book of poems based on the gospels as reading matter for a trip to Spain. She also gives him a journal in which to begin writing his account of the eighth deadly sin, but the quality of his first sentences causes him to despair because they don't match up to the elegance of Sir Thomas Browne. How many Upper Peninsula Michigan ex-cops read *Religio Medici* in their earlier lives and can recall it in their sixties? And which of them would turn to Djuna Barnes's *Nightwood*[2] for further stylistic help? Something very odd is going on here, and while many fans of Jim Harrison read him for what they take to be his own quirky intellectualism placed in the mouth of unlikely characters, this is just too easy a judgment. We need to ask, in Coleridge's terms, what act of the secondary imagination is Harrison

---

[2] Djuna Barnes, *Nightwood* (New York: New Directions, 1961).

engaged in here? We are interested not in him but in the work of the imagination present in the text. What, we might ask in other words, is our takeaway?

Grace and the Seven Deadly Sins

Karl Rahner's theological anthropology is the best way into understanding what is going on in *The Big Seven*, and our starting point might be with his judgment that "radical dependence on . . . [God] increases in direct, and not in inverse proportion with genuine self-coherence before him."[3] Putting this in slightly less Rahnerian language, his point is that the more we become more fully ourselves, the more truly dependent on God we are. This kind of dependence on God is not servile but something more like the unity demonstrated in Christian theology in the figure of Christ, at once the perfect instantiation of what it is to be a human being and at the same time the presence of God in history. The kind of dependence that makes Christ who he is will also be the kind of dependence on God that makes us who we are, not because we are Christians but because we are human beings, and not because we know about this ontological dependence on God for our human completeness but because our growth toward "genuine self-coherence" is in fact our growth into God, whether we know it or not.

Rahner's understanding of the identity between self-coherence and union with God is a reflection of his complex but important notion of "the supernatural existential." Because we are created by God in the divine image and likeness and because the model of the divine-human relationship is Jesus Christ, we have to think of the human being as possessed of a sort of ontological capacity for relationship to God. It is not part of our nature, because it is a gift of God, but because the gift comes with creation, our natures do not exist apart from

---

[3] Karl Rahner, "Current Problems in Christology," in *Theological Investigations* 1 (Baltimore, MD: Helicon, 1965), 149–200, here 162.

the ontological orientation to the divine mystery. Relatedness to God is a direct consequence of God's self-communication to us, which we can certainly reject but which always remains on offer. There is no such thing as a "natural" person who is entirely devoid of grace. Nature is always already graced and "nature" alone is a "residue concept," that is, notional but not real. We can conceive of nature alone but we cannot ever encounter it. Wherever we go, whoever we meet, we somehow encounter in the grace of God the divine spark that is in all of us. And because a human being can reject God or reject self-coherence, which amounts to the same thing, but can never destroy the relatedness to God or the connection between self-coherence and human fulfillment, even the damned in hell are still somehow graced. Of course, the evident nonsensical character of *that* claim leads quickly to the conclusion that hell itself is a notional rather than a real entity, or the weaker version, hell exists but it is empty. Nevertheless, Rahner insists on our freedom to reject God's self-communication.

The majority of people of faith fail to understand the idea of "grace," or perhaps more commonly think of it as something added on to the human person because either of what we do (Catholics' good works) or of something God does (Protestant faith). So the erroneous understanding from which much else follows is that we start as a kind of *tabula rasa*, upon which grace is subsequently laid, either as God's free act of love or because of some access we have to special sources of grace. Catholics might sometimes think of the seven sacraments in this way. If we focus on grace in this way then of course it is not difficult to divide human beings into good people and bad people or to see "mortal sin" as destroying any connection to God. The same distinction inevitably leads to a separation between the sacred and the secular and a vision of the community of faith as a community of the blessed set apart from a sinful world. None of this can stand up to the inspiration of great literature.

In serious fiction we are presented with human beings of such complexity that the simplistic distinctions between good and evil or sacred and secular cannot stand. When people of faith read this kind of literature they are tutored by it to eschew all the us/them oppositions with which traditional religion is so often bedecked and to think again about divine grace. When secular people read the same books they are encouraged to accept the complex and often ambiguous expressions of human goodness. And when we invoke the understanding of grace that depends on Karl Rahner's rethinking of Aquinas, we can see that divine grace and human goodness are inextricably interlinked. But further, we also have to accept that the already-graced nature that is the only kind of human being we can ever encounter, persists also not only in sinners, for that would be all of us, but even in those we might think of as evil or depraved. If it did not, God would stop loving them, and that cannot happen.

While it would be a mistake to imagine that we need to know about Karl Rahner in order to grasp what is going on in serious fiction, it is true that Rahner and Harrison can illuminate one another. In the first place, grasping this notion of grace makes it much easier to see how the characters that fill the pages of *The Big Seven* cannot be divided into good and bad people, though they certainly do good and bad things. But second and more significant, the work of Jim Harrison forecloses our option to think of any single human being as *either* bad *or* good. So while knowing Rahner can illuminate the complex world of Harrison, reading Harrison can illustrate the point that Rahner is making. Imagine you were teaching an undergraduate class on grace. Do you think it would be more helpful for your students to begin with extracts from the *Summa Theologica* of Aquinas and some of volume 1 of Rahner's *Theological Investigations,* or to offer them a mystery story set in the wilds of northern Michigan? If the protagonist of *The Big Seven* is a little too much like their grandfathers for his sexual appetites to seem anything other than "yucky," he is also a recognizable example of the tension between temptation, generosity, and human kindness that afflicts all of us some of the time, and that is not respective of age.

Is There Grace in Taulkinham?

Wise Blood[4] is one of the most challenging of novels about which to reflect theologically, though its author was well known for her quite traditional Catholicism and the story revolves around the meaning of salvation. The difficulty arises from the fact that practically no one in the story seems to be anything other than morally repellent. The reader of *Wise Blood* is taunted by the story, pushed and prodded to make some sense of the events, frankly, without much luck. The only religion we encounter in the small southern town in which the book is set is either bizarre—"The Church without Christ"—or frankly hypocritical. If God's grace is at work in Taulkinham, it is practically impossible to see. Meanness of spirit seems to rule over all other human sentiments. And yet something draws us in and on.

If making complete sense of this story is challenging, then its very murkiness is the vehicle by which we, the readers, create our own aesthetic objects. Because something is dark it does not mean that it is beyond the scope of our imaginations and, in fact, it may stimulate them. In the opening pages we meet the central character, Hazel Motes, who seems mysterious, hopeless, and more than a little chilling, but nevertheless we are pushed by the events that follow to consider and reconsider his motivations. There is surely something in his life before we meet him that has created in him the strange set of beliefs and behavior we encounter. Traveling by train to

---

[4] Flannery O'Connor, *Wise Blood* (New York: Farrar, Straus and Cudahy, 1962).

Taulkinham to "do some things I have never done before," he asks the woman sitting opposite him, Mrs. Wally Bee Hitchcock, if she thinks she has been redeemed. Later, in the dining car across from a younger woman thoughtlessly blowing smoke in his face, he tells her that if she has been redeemed, he wouldn't want to be. Redemption is clearly on his mind, but he says he doesn't believe in Jesus. And the first thing he does when his train arrives is find a distinctly unsavory prostitute with whom to "do some things" he has "never done before." A strange kind of preacher he is, though he always wanted to be a preacher and he wears clothes and a hat that announce him as a preacher, even if he has forgotten to remove the price tag from his suit. In the cab to the prostitute's place of business ("Mrs. Leora Watts . . . the friendliest bed in town") he denies to the driver that he is a preacher, no doubt because the driver knows about Mrs. Leora Watts. The cabbie turns out to be something of a theologian: "It ain't nobody perfect on this green earth of God's, preachers nor nobody else. And you can tell people better how terrible sin is if you know from your own personal experience."

From the beginning, Motes's eyes are a center of attention. Mrs. Hitchcock notices his eyes, "the color of pecan shells and set in deep sockets. . . . Their settings were so deep that they seemed, to her, almost like passages leading somewhere." By the end of the story the failed preacher, Hazel Motes, has killed a man with his car. He drives out of town and has his car destroyed by a police officer because he doesn't have a license. Walking back to his lodging house he picks up lime and blinds himself. His eyesight destroyed, he walks everywhere with glass and rocks in his shoes in order, he tells Mrs. Flood, his landlady, "to pay," though to pay for what he doesn't seem entirely sure. She thinks that he "had the look of seeing something," and when she eventually sits beside his dead body and looks into the wounded eye sockets that "seemed to lead into the dark tunnel where he had disappeared," sadly, "she couldn't see anything." Finally, she "sat staring with her eyes shut, into his eyes," and "felt as if she had finally got to the beginning of something she couldn't begin."

The one character in the story who elicits anything like sympathy is the developmentally challenged Enoch Emery, looking "like a friendly hound dog with light mange." For a time he follows Motes around, eventually escaping Motes and the novel itself by donning a gorilla suit and fleeing into the distance, to what future it is impossible to predict. Motes's temporary girlfriend, Sabbath Lily Hawkes, is at times a pathetic waif under the thumb of her father, a preacher who pretends to be blind, at other times a morally compromised seeker after security at any price. The father is a confidence-trickster. That about exhausts the significant figures, though the minor ones are drawn with exquisitely realistic speech, even if it accompanies fantastic hopes and ideas. It is as if O'Connor has observed reality so carefully and transmuted it into something utterly beyond realism.

Too seamy to be a fantasy, *Wise Blood* is a fictional nightmare, a kind of perverse *Alice in Wonderland*, where human hopes are dashed and God or grace seem not to be present. In Taulkinham everything is reversed. The blind preacher is actually a fake who can see perfectly well behind his dark glasses. Hazel Motes cannot see while he has his sight, but somehow once he is blinded he comes to see something that previously escaped him, if only that he must "pay." Perhaps he is thinking of the murder, perhaps the lesser sins that he is guilty of, perhaps even preaching a church without Jesus Christ. He can't preach anymore because he doesn't have the time, and he hopes that the dead are blind because, "if there's no bottom in your eyes, they hold more."

Anyone with any familiarity with the Christian gospels will hear lots of echoes here, though the more secular reader may be struggling. Didn't Jesus come so that "the blind may see," and didn't he come "to call sinners"? Isn't it the lost sheep or the prodigal son who is the one for whom he goes out of his way? Jesus confronts people with paradox, culminating in the final paradox that the grain of wheat must fall to the ground and die if it is to bear fruit, that through death comes life. As he leaves the house alive for the last time Mrs. Flood asks Motes if he is planning to go to another city, only to be told that "there's no other house nor no other city." And she wants him to stay because if she is going to be blind when she is dead, "then who better to guide her than a blind man?"

If some readers will struggle with the difficult relationship between the truths of the Gospel and the life and death of Hazel Motes, while others will see at least a kind of wisdom in his more gnomic utterances, every reader of this text is summoned to engage the complex metaphors of sight and blindness and of life and death. Neither Christian or any other kind of believers nor secular people will be at any advantage here. Both kinds of people will struggle with the unfamiliar challenges of stretching the metaphors in O'Connor's way, and neither group is offered any kind of comfortable resolution. This text is neither atheistic nor fideistic, but it tantalizes both kinds of reader with both possibilities. Just what did Hazel Motes think he was doing, in life and in death? In the space between the reader and the text something surely is working its way out. It remains an open question, however, whether it is good or evil that at least temporarily triumphs. Mrs. Flood's venality seems to be shot through with at least a measure of concern, even compassion, for the blind man of whom she is taking advantage, as she overcharges him and steals his money. And Motes evidently has some sense of guilt or he would not be "paying," though O'Connor gives little away about his deeper thoughts and to the end he seems disinclined toward the standard conversion experience, telling Mrs. Flood that if she believed in Jesus she "wouldn't be so good." Motes's death does not bring closure.

The Big Seven *and* Wise Blood *Compared: What Is "the Matter"?*

At first sight these two novels have very little in common and many distinct differences. The world of *The Big Seven* is one of violence and terror but also of fishing and ornithology, while *Wise Blood* is a place of gloom relieved only by the flashes of humor in dialogue and commentary. Harrison's book moves along with a mystery at its center that may not be its true heart but that quickens the action and provokes our curiosity. It is also the background against which the homespun wisdom and wry commentary of its central character is set in relief. There is a mystery of sorts in *Wise Blood*, though more of the nature of puzzling over what will happen to Motes in the end than solving the traditional whodunit. Rape and sexual abuse abound in the Upper Peninsula Michigan of the Ames clan, but the sexual gratification doled out amply to Sunderson is always affectionate, if not always wise. In contrast, sex in Motes's Taulkinham is either a tawdry mercantile exchange or a ruse to snare a partner. Love and affection are in short supply in *Wise Blood*, in overflowing abundance in *The Big Seven*. O'Connor's book is saying, in effect, "Here is something really horrible, and you figure out how God is at work here, if at all." Harrison's text shows instead how the seven deadly sins are inextricably intermingled in the world, in the family, and maybe even in every individual in the story, though in different measures in each of them.

Above and beyond the evident differences in style and story, the two books are at one in their capacity to push the reader beyond the surface story toward, if not into, an altogether different realm of reflection. For all their differences and their fantastical elements, they exhibit realism about human beings in the hardscrabble struggle for life and love. They are mostly about failure, even if the failures in the one are more all-encompassing than in the other. But both of them inflect the failures in such a way that the reader grasps that there may be something beyond failure. It will always be a maybe, because each in its own way is realistic about human life and profoundly undogmatic, eschewing all forms of didacticism. Hazel Motes remains Jesus-haunted to the end, determined to deny him while sensing Jesus "moving from tree to tree in the back of his mind, a wild ragged figure motioning to come off into the dark where he was not sure of his footing." It would have been so easy for O'Connor to insert a phrase or two in the final pages to prove a religious point. But she is too good for that, leaving it to the reader to decide if and how grace is at work in Motes's final days. In *The Big Seven* the ambivalence is more evident and the reader must come up with a balanced judgment not only about Sunderson, to whom we naturally feel well-disposed, since his human weaknesses are matched by his growth toward "self-coherence," but also about a world in which the Ameses have flourished for quite some time.

When these texts challenge the reader not only to go beyond the surface but even to go beyond the "beyond the surface," they bring us back to thoughts about what Henry James called "the matter" and what is for Coleridge the content of the primary imagination and what, for the person of faith, impinges on the mystery of the meaning of the whole that is often called God or the sacred. The human imagination never draws a line, but it does come upon a boundary or what Karl Rahner calls a horizon. There is something beyond the horizon that indeed creates the horizon that limits our grasp of the knowable, but what the nature of that something beyond really is will not be accessible to us in our terrestrial existence. And yet we would have to say that it must be, to use Erik Erikson's famous term, "friendly," because it is the condition of possibility not only of the goodness and graciousness of this world but also of the imagination that is both bounded by finitude and yet straining to get beyond it. The secular reader will recognize the same human urge to look beyond what there actually is to see, and the work of the novel is to persuade such a reader that the simple dismissal of these urges of the imagination is too reductive. Otherwise, creativity is just a sham.

Returning now to *The Wounded Angel*, we can look at it in one further way as an illustration of the reader's task in the encounter with fiction to create the aesthetic object. There is a picture before our eyes, and we can easily describe what we see there. There is a multiplicity of ways in which we can explain what is happening, starting from a very pedestrian refusal to pick up on signals in the painting, so that we will see it as a fancy dress accident in a local park. But the more we examine it, as we saw at the beginning of this chapter, the more there is that challenges us to look deeper. What is so striking about this picture and what it has in common with great art in general and great fiction in particular is, as we have said so many times, it means more than it says and perhaps than it knows it means. We can argue about whether all serious fiction qualifies as "classic," and it would perhaps cheapen the term to defend such a claim. But we can say that serious literature approaches classic status to the degree that it demonstrates its ability to *mean*, beyond its time, beyond its space, and beyond its author. The one thing we might want to add is that what makes the great work of art is the way in which the reader or observer creatively appropriates something of the ambiguity it contains, while all the readers there ever were can never fully exhaust its depths.

Chapter Eight

The Communion of Saints

"Goodness existed; that was the new knowledge his
terror had to blow itself quite out to let him see."

(W. H. Auden)

"My books are about terror. That brooding terror curled deep
down inside us. But more than that, more than murder, more than
all the rancid emotions and actions, my books are about goodness.
And kindness. About choices. About friendship and belonging.
And love. Enduring love."

(Louise Penny)

One of the most important theological tropes of the Catholic
tradition is that of the communion of saints. Traditionally it
refers to the entire community of the holy people of God, those
in heaven, those in purgatory, and those still living on earth.
Protestant traditions have had some problems with this feature
of Catholic theology, particularly the attendant belief that those
in heaven can be prayed to for intercession and that those on
earth can pray for those in purgatory. Nevertheless, the central
idea of the communion of saints is not in dispute.[1] While not

---

[1] See, for example, the early work of Dietrich Bonhoeffer, *The Communion
of Saints: A Dogmatic Inquiry into the Sociology of the Church* (London: Forgotten
Books, 2015).

all Christians accept the idea of intercessory prayer, the idea that all believers are bound together in one holy community is not controversial, though that does not mean that all Christian traditions are in agreement about what constitutes a "believer."

More recent theological reflection on the communion of saints, particularly the work of Elizabeth Johnson, has expanded enormously the range of the communion of saints, not only to incorporate the righteous of all faiths and none, but also to include the whole of creation.[2] So while for much of its history and among many controversialists the main purpose of the idea of a communion of saints was that of exclusion, today the doctrine in at least some hands has reached a point of radical inclusion. Indeed, one might usefully parallel the development of the doctrine to a similar development in the idea of hell. We no longer share Dante's generous inclusion of so many people in hell and wonder if anyone at all is there or, if so, just how few there might be. In similar fashion, if all the righteous are to be included in the communion of saints, and so long as we recognize that "the righteous" are also sinners, then how many can we truly exclude? The souls in purgatory are there *because* of their sinfulness, though they are surely part of the communion of saints. And the communion of saints on earth is the body of the righteous, sinners yet redeemed.

We can get a better grasp of the contemporary meaning of the communion of saints if we relate it to Rahner's understanding of grace, which we explored in the previous chapter. Both doctrines in their present forms reflect an understanding of the implications of the doctrine of creation. Once we abandon any notion of grace as something simply added to nature

---

[2] Elizabeth Johnson, *Friends of God and Prophets: A Feminist Theological Reading of the Communion of Saints* (New York: Bloomsbury, 1999), and *Truly Our Sister: A Theology of Mary in the Communion of Saints* (New York: Bloomsbury, 2006).

and see that nature is always already graced, then the default condition of all human beings, so to speak, is that of being graced with the gift of God's love in and through their human natures. The nonhuman world does not know sin and is thereby always and forever graced, though harm can come to it extrinsically, from the sinful predatory activity of human beings, selfishly instrumentalizing the natural world to their "needs."[3] But human beings are in the more complicated and more responsible situation of being called to live their lives in a struggle between the angels of their better nature and the other kind. Sin and grace are evident in each of us, throughout our lives, in greater or lesser measure depending to some degree on circumstances and to a greater degree on what Rahner referred to as "genuine self-coherence."

Once we accept the idea that all human beings are born into an always/already graced nature, then it is theologically problematic to define the communion of saints in such a way that it excludes some, perhaps the majority, and includes only the favored few. Either we are all children of God, or we are not. It cannot be that some of us are and some are not. If it is possible to argue that some have a different relationship than others to the creator God, then it cannot be that the accident of their birth makes them more faithful or more favored.[4] When God makes human beings in the divine image, then it follows that "self-coherence" is becoming closer to the divine image and that this itself amounts to becoming more and more fully and richly human. Growth into full humanity is by no means the prized possession of the Christian or any other religious tradition. It is the challenge of living that all human beings

[3] Elizabeth Johnson, *Ask the Beasts: Darwin and the God of Love* (New York: Bloomsbury, 2015).

[4] Juan Luis Segundo's distinction between the community of redemption and the community of revelation sees the latter as a Christian characteristic not shared by the human race at large, but this is a mark of responsibility, not of favor and still less of distinction or virtue.

share. Indeed, responding to this challenge seems to be very much what Rahner had in mind when he argued that God's salvific will means that everyone in all places and at all times is offered somehow the gift of salvation in Jesus Christ.[5] When we respond to the demand placed on us to grow in love and hence in our humanity, then we are "saved," then we are part of the communion of saints. Only those few, if any, who formally reject the call to love and humanity stand outside this communion. Not to believe in God does not shut you out of salvation. Not to believe in love and humanity just might.

The expansion of our understanding of what it means to be saved, what it means to be born always/already graced, and what it means in consequence to be part of the communion of saints has to revolutionize how we think of the workings of serious literature. Whenever fiction explores the complexity and ambiguity of the human condition, it is engaging with the mystery of sin and grace. It is immaterial whether the author or the reader is familiar or comfortable with these categories. To read great fiction is to be tutored in the human condition. The education of our sensibilities brings us to the brink of the matter or the mystery, without ever grasping it fully. In this sense, the act of reading at this level is exactly parallel to the act of faith, which also brings us, for Christians through the encounter with Christ, to the brink of the mystery of the otherness of God, though never past that point this side of eternity. Once again, we encounter the correspondence: literature can enlighten the religious imagination, in this case can broaden our appreciation of the mystery of grace, and at the same time quicken in the secular reader a sense of the "more" that just might lie beyond the text. In the space between, the reader constructs the aesthetic object, which is at once revealed also as the religious object.

[5] Karl Rahner, "Christianity and the Non-Christian Religions," in *Theological Investigations* 5 (Baltimore, MD: Helicon, 1966), 115–34.

Modern fiction provides us with a kind of catechesis in what it means to be holy in the world today and, of course, in what it means to fail to be holy. Being holy and being fully human are much the same, and both are more or less identical to what Christians will call growing in the image and likeness of God. But whatever words one uses to describe what is happening, serious fiction tutors us in the multitude of ways in which people struggle with the tension between sin and grace. The context of the individual quest is the commonality of the communion of saints, which again is not at all what one would expect in traditional religious categories. We can find the struggle for holiness in the most surprising places, and we can see it worked out in the unlikeliest of fictional contexts. If we want a fictional image for the predicament of the person of faith whose imagination is being stretched to see holiness in a different light, we need look no further than Mrs. Turpin in Flannery O'Connor's late story, "Revelation."[6] After a particularly hard day marked by her limited perspective and settled convictions about life, this deeply conventional woman has her world turned upside down by a vision of "a vast horde of souls . . . tumbling towards heaven." Those leading the way are the "trash," as she referred to them, black and white both, "and battalions of lunatics shouting and clapping and leaping like frogs." Her own kind, the good and respectable people are there too, but at the rear of the procession: "They were marching behind the others with great dignity, accountable as they had always been for good order and common sense and respectable behavior." And "they alone were on key." There is room for everyone, O'Connor is saying, but the first shall be last and the last shall be first. And as for the respectable people, "even their virtues were being burned away." It would be such a mistake to assume that there is only one way to self-coherence

---

[6] Flannery O'Connor, "Revelation," in *Everything That Rises Must Converge* (New York: Farrar, Straus and Giroux, 1965), 191–218.

and to assume that the best way to think about the challenges of being fully human requires religious language. Perhaps fiction can be equally useful. Perhaps it can sometimes be more useful.

What Is Holiness Today?

Classical hagiography provides us with little assistance in thinking about what it means to be holy. No doubt the objects of saints' lives were in their time models of personal sanctity, but the conventions of the genre of hagiography for the most part preclude any reference to anything other than heroic virtue and ascetical practices. True, there are some lives that at least touch on the time before conversion, though often enough conversion in pious religious fiction was never something necessary. The greatness of Augustine's *Confessions* is that he was not afraid to recognize his earlier sinfulness, even though we might think that stealing pears falls quite a way down the list of serious sins. But a better and earlier example of the genre and how it treats the early life of the saint can be found in St. Athanasius's *Life of Anthony*,[7] the story of the putative founder of monasticism. While most of the tale is taken up with the teachings and miracles of the fully formed monk, there is a short initial consideration of what led the young man to embrace the ascetical life. Even as a child he was distinguished from his peers, for "neither as a child was he idle . . . but was both obedient to his father and mother and attentive to what was read. . . . And though as a child brought up in moderate affluence, he did not trouble his parents for varied or luxurious fare, nor was this a source of pleasure to him." At the age of eighteen or thereabouts his father and mother died and he was left to care for his sister. One day he was thinking

[7] Athanasius, *The Life of Antony and the Letter to Marcellinus* (Mahwah, NJ: Paulist Press, 1979).

about how the apostles left all and followed Jesus, and, turning into a church, heard the gospel of the rich young man: "If thou wouldst be perfect, go and sell that thou hast and give to the poor; and come follow Me and thou shalt have treasure in heaven." So he gives away his possessions, puts his little sister into safekeeping in a convent, and takes off for the desert. In the body of the story Anthony is tempted by demons but never succumbs.

The story of Anthony neither models holiness for us today nor edifies us, because it does not seem to correspond to what we take to be human. It is formulaic, lacking the essentials of humanity. People are just not like that, not even the saintly ones. Holiness as a point at which some of us may arrive is a dynamic process throughout the whole of life. If we seek it out, it may escape us. And growth in holiness surely requires a struggle with the normal human passions, one which the modern sensibility is fairly sure will have involved making a mistake or two and learning from those errors. Indeed, it is probably fair to say that most of our contemporaries would consider learning from failings, even from sins, to be a sign of growth toward sanctity. No one is born that way. Fiction thrives on the assumption that virtue (and maybe even vice) is not interesting or faithful to real life if it is not a dynamic process of growth and that in the daily struggle between their best and worst impulses genuinely interesting characters come into being.

For a classic text illustrating the requirement that virtue be seen as emerging from a struggle with sinfulness there can be no better example than Graham Greene's *The Power and the Glory*,[8] a book about an alcoholic priest in Mexico who believes himself damned for fathering a child whom he loves and consequently whose conception he cannot repent. But what makes the book especially valuable in this context is that Greene inter-

[8] Graham Greene, *The Power and the Glory* (London: Penguin Classics, 2003).

sperses his text with extracts from the worst of hagiography. While the unnamed priest is struggling to save his life, a woman reads to her family: "Young Juan from his earliest years was noted for humility and piety. Other boys might be rough and revengeful; young Juan followed the precept of Our Lord and turned the other cheek." And much more of the same. At the end of the book the whiskey priest awaits his execution thinking, "what an impossible fellow I am . . . and how useless." He felt "an immense disappointment because he had to go to God empty-handed." But the hagiography of the young seminarian Juan has him meeting the firing squad with "a smile of complete adoration and happiness," calling out "Hail, Christ the King." Here is pious nonsense competing with harsh reality, but few readers will miss the message that the whiskey priest, for all his failings, is the true saint.

This story and countless others make two important points for us: that the quest for holiness, the wish to be "a saint," is one language for the more universal human desire for integrity and that the fulfilment of this desire can be accomplished only in the context of community or, if you will, communion. The whiskey priest is not the best judge of his own progress toward God. Only the readers, who see him in the wider context of his own life, are well-placed to estimate the kind of man he is and to discriminate among the many diverse judgments that other characters in the story make about him. And if for much of the story we follow his own reflections, of even greater importance are the judgments that others are making about him. As the reader enters the story and inevitably is led to an assessment of the central character, deeper reflections naturally emerge on the relationship between strength and weakness and their sources, and constrain the careful reader to internalize what there is here to learn about the challenge of life, or as Albert Camus saw it (in patriarchal language, admittedly), "to be a man."

When we recognize the predicament of a central character in a fiction we are drawn into the creation of the aesthetic object, as Wolfgang Iser referred to the process of imaginative appropriation of the story. In appropriating the story, to a degree we personalize it. We make it our own. Because each of us who reads the same story brings to it a different background and life situation, each of us will create an aesthetic object that bears some considerable similarities to those produced by other readers but that can never be identical. In reading *The Power and the Glory* every careful reader comes to some kind of conclusion about the human worth of the whiskey priest and, indeed, of other central characters, most important, the revolutionary lieutenant who is the priest's principal adversary. To say we come to a conclusion is not at all to assert, however, that there is closure. What makes great fiction is precisely its open-endedness, its dependence on metaphor and symbol that of their nature contain a surplus of meaning. Thus, it is most commonly great fiction to which we return again and again, though not simply to repeat the experience. Or, if we reread to repeat the pleasure of a first encounter, we surely encounter greater depths or new insights. In this particular novel by Graham Greene, and any other of similar or greater stature, the skill of the author produced a text that inspires the readers not merely to enjoy or to try to understand but also and more important to nudge up against that horizon beyond which lies something finally true about human life. But this is a something which we will never totally grasp.

There is a second good example of the kind of challenge encountered in *The Power and the Glory* in Shusaku Endo's novel *Silence*, which anyone who has come to it after the Greene novel must see as a variation on the same theme, an homage to Greene and, frankly, showing some dependence on the earlier work. Superficially, they are quite similar. Both stories have as their central character a priest who is betrayed by a dubious and disreputable companion. Both take place in a situation where the church is being persecuted. Both priests encounter a wily adversary with whom they dispute. And in the end both of them must face questions of the struggle for integrity in the face of their own human weaknesses. But there is one huge difference between them. While the whiskey priest is placed before a firing squad, the Jesuit Fr. Rodrigues lives out his life in a comfortable but arguably dishonorable retirement.

The genius of Endo's novel lies in his willingness to take the question of integrity or holiness a step beyond where Graham Greene left it. In some ways *The Power and the Glory* is a simple tale. Few readers finish the book without seeing that for all his human failings the whisky priest is truly admirable. As a novel, it is a textbook case for understanding the movements of sin and grace within one human being. It surely invites the reader into deeper reflections. But *Silence* presents us with a depiction of a far more profound internal struggle, and one that the reader may find extremely difficult to judge. Fr. Rodrigues must choose between staunchly affirming his faith in God and condemning many innocents to horrible suffering, or saving them by publicly abjuring his faith, with all that this will mean for demoralizing the very people he is being asked to save. If he abandons his faith, it may lead them to renounce their own, since the priest is their model of closeness to God. If he maintains his faith, they will die in excruciating suffering. The choice he will make in the end will depend on his understanding of the passion of Christ. He will, inevitably, act on the implied question beloved of evangelicals, "what would Jesus do?"

Both *The Power and the Glory* and *Silence* explore the delicate and troubling challenge of faith, but each in its own way presses on toward the matter, the inaccessible answer to the necessary question, what lies beyond faith? This is *the* religious question, but it also has its secular counterpart. While a person of faith stakes the meaning of this life on the hope of something infinitely good that lies beyond it, the secular mind does not have that luxury. On the other hand, the absence of what we would normally call faith in the secular person's self-understanding makes even more insistent the question of "why?" Altruism must be its own justification. At the same time, the modern believer who lives *etsi deus non daretur* derives the strength to believe in an age of doubt from the way in which faith nourishes a commitment to the meaning of *this* life. And this, of course, forces faith into an even more mysterious position in the life of the believer than it might have held in more traditional times. To express the contrast crudely: whereas faith has meant for most of Christian history a personal commitment to the one who will save us for the life to come, today it is more a personal relationship with Christ that sheds light on how to live now, in which any sense of a "beyond" is consigned to trust in a mystery that we cannot and even should not explore in the here and now.

In an odd way, *Silence* and to a lesser degree *The Power and the Glory* bring together Christian faith and secular altruism. If altruism is best understood as selfless concern for the good of others, concern that motivates the altruist even if the actions that follow are harmful to the self, then it cannot be said that Christians are altruistic. In fact, no religious believers act purely altruistically, since their actions are motivated by commitment to a scheme of things in which their selfless actions bring some kind of reward, however unfocused that might be. The one who simply does good in order to get to heaven is not acting morally at all, in the Kantian sense, but acting to win a prize. The one who follows the selflessness of Jesus even to the point of death is certainly acting more admirably than one whose good deed is motivated by crude self-concern. But can this ever be *as* admirable as the purely altruistic action, done without hope of any reward?

Both Rodrigues and the whiskey priest are faced with a situation in which the altruistic action seems to conflict with what their religious belief demands of them. So, Greene's whiskey priest lives his life in terror of damnation, while Rodrigues has to consider an act that may turn a blameless life into one bereft of contact with God. When we meet the priest, never named, we discover that in a brief lapse in commitment to his celibacy he has fathered a child. He loves this child so deeply, despite the fact that she seems to be deeply unlovable, that he cannot bring himself to confess his "mortal sin." Thus he lives and will die damned for his commitment to the love he has for his child, or so he believes. Rodrigues, on the other hand, is someone whom we admire for his religious commitment and his bravery through the greater part of the novel only to find in the end that he is faced with a choice between what seems like integrity and its abandonment. The priest chooses the altruistic action of care for another despite the most profound kind of harm to himself, while Rodrigues considers an altruistic act that appears to entail the end of his faith in God.

Both of these novels in their different ways pursue the careful reader into reflection on the paradoxes of belief, while at the same time they enlighten the secular reader with a deeper sense of the kinship that may exist between such a reader and someone whose religious faith seems to be so alien. The whiskey priest and Rodrigues are evidently men of faith, but their lives are severely compromised by circumstance and perhaps by their own struggles with the paschal mystery of death and new life. In unlikely ways they encourage reflection on the meaning of holiness in our world. Could it be a holy act to die in mortal sin, or could a selfless act somehow cancel that sin? And might it be a sign of holiness to abjure faith in the service of others? These situations call on people of faith to enlarge their understandings of what faith might mean, even at the cost of comfort. But at the same time and in much the same way, readers for whom faith in the usual sense of the word is not an option cannot but empathize with the predicament of a saintly sinner and a sinful saint. And in doing so, both the believer and nonbeliever are brought closer to the horizon beyond which lies an answer to the relationship between faith in God and selfless love of the other. The "matter" hovers just out of eyesight, but it is there nonetheless.

Life and Death in Bailey's Café

Gloria Naylor's novel, *Bailey's Café*,[9] pushes the envelope about as far as it can be pushed, over the question of what holiness might mean today, of who is a saint and who is a sinner. There are bad people in this book, no doubt, but they are the minor characters. The principals are for the most part deeply sinful and recognizably holy. *Bailey's Café* is some kind of halfway house, though whether between life and death or heaven and hell is a matter for speculation. "Bailey" (we never learn his real name) returns from the Pacific War in 1945 a disillusioned man, and his reveries are interrupted in a dreamlike sequence as "a hand reached through the fog" and touched his shoulder with the words, "There's a customer waiting." The speaker is his wife and business partner, Nadine, whom he had managed to meet one day at a baseball game by dint of slopping his ice cream down the back of her dress. These two run the café in a very unorthodox manner, never sure quite what they will charge, with only one dish available each weekday and whatever you want on weekends. And the customers "don't come for the food and don't come for the atmosphere." In fact, says Bailey, the sloppiness of the service and the doubtful quality of the food are intended to stop the clientele "thinking we're actually in the business of running a café." More mysterious still, one day the café is there, another day not, but in truth, he says, "we're only here when they need us." It also shows up in various cities, always between Eve's boarding house and Gabe's pawnshop, though the latter is never open

---

[9] Gloria Naylor, *Bailey's Café* (New York: Harcourt Brace Jovanovich, 1992).

and always directs potential customers down the street to the café.

One way or another, the customers who show up at the café are all at the end of their tether. The café is a place "to take a breather for a while." If it weren't there, explains Bailey, "the edge of the world . . . could be the end of the world." So in they come, one after another, each with a challenging history. There's Sadie the genteel alcoholic, who sells her body to pay the rent but only asks for exactly what she needs, even if it is as little as ten cents. Finding the café and the gentle Iceman Jones, she is on the verge of something better as they stand at the back of the café. "Since the place sits right on the margin between the edge of the world and infinite possibility, the back door opens out to a void." You can dance, or you can fall. Then there is Eve, who escapes a brutal childhood to make a fortune in New Orleans and returns to set up the boarding house next door for women, one that has lots of "gentlemen callers." They are all obliged to bring flowers, but it's hard not to see it as a brothel. But not too fast, since Esther is next on the scene, a woman who has been kept captive from the age of twelve and subjected to regular sadomasochistic rape in a dark cellar. Freed, she enters Eve's boarding house, where she is given the dark basement room to receive her gentlemen callers. But they must bring white roses. Eve is also host to Mary, nicknamed Peaches, who can only end the cycle of abusive sex by mutilating her face with a beer can opener. She too needs flowers from her callers, and as time goes on they become more expensive and the visits last longer. Eve tells Peaches' father, "Go home, my friend, . . . and I'll return your daughter to you whole." Soon there will be a request for flowers unavailable at any price, and a special man who will understand, and "there'll be no one else waiting." There are many more characters: Jesse Bell, whom Eve is trying to wean cold turkey from heroin addiction, or Mariam, a young Ethiopian Jew who has undergone genital mutilation and is now pregnant, though she insists "no man has ever touched me." And then there is Stanley Beck-wourth Booker T. Washington Carver, a highly educated African American man who cross-dresses as "Miss Maple" and serves as the bouncer at Eve's boarding house. Having discovered that the color of his skin was preventing him from getting jobs for which he was well qualified, he decided to go to the interviews in women's dresses. They were more comfortable in the summer heat, and they made a point about looking beyond the appearances. Nothing to lose, because he wasn't going to get the job anyway.

Sadie (Sarah), Eve, Esther, Mary, Jesse Bell (Jezebel?), Mariam, Gabe the pawnshop owner. The long list of biblical names cannot be coincidental, though this is not a religious book in any obvious sense. And yet it is surely about the struggle to overcome the past and to find healing if not redemption. Like *The Big Seven* and *Wise Blood*, like the books of Greene and Endo, all the characters escape easy categorization. There is no simple dichotomy of good and evil. Each has a struggle going on within, and what makes *Bailey's Café* so remarkable is that the rag-tag community of Eve, Bailey, Nadine, and Gabe provide a potentially healing location. No one is entirely lost here, and even the two characters who seem to lose in fact do not, because one relinquishes self out of love for another, while the second dies in the act of bringing about new life. Not bad for a cast of characters most of whom the respectable people would "pass by on the other side."

There are several characteristics of this novel that amplify and shed further light on the relationship between fiction and faith that we have been considering. Faith is aided by fiction in fiction's consistent orientation to complexity and ambiguity, to a metaphorical structure that resists dichotomies, still more dogmatic utterances. And fiction is brought through its own creativity to the horizon of mystery where, like people of faith, even secular readers may sense something more to which they are oriented, even if it is a mystery beyond human comprehension. So in *Bailey's Café* we encounter a world in which judging others seems not to occur, in which all individuals are working through their own challenges in the face of a common existential reality, in which success is measured modestly, and in which this personal struggle brings each person toward, even to the verge of, a deeper, more challenging, and even fearsome beyond.

The whole book is hopeful and tragic at one and the same time. Is Sadie a prostitute and an alcoholic or a gentlewoman? Both, but Iceman Jones tells a funny story and she responds with a laugh "like music," so that "the whole café stood still . . . in the presence of something that beautiful and rare." Dancing on the edge by the back door, Jones leans into her and "Sadie had her first real kiss." Jones proposes, and in the saddest moment in the book she turns him down, perhaps knowing that she is too far gone in alcohol to do him justice. Is Esther winning or losing as she receives one man after another for sex in the basement? Well, she is the one who is in control, she demands the flowers, and, whatever else it is, it is not the abuse she survived for many years. Jesse Bell is still on heroin, being treated by Eve with the worst kind of tough love, in training to see if she can ever free herself or if she will remain where Eve is constantly reminding her she is, in hell. But Esther and Jesse and all the rest are present to celebrate the birth of Mariam's baby boy with dancing in the café. Some of these people are winning the battle, others are losing, all are in flux. Like the world itself, Bailey seems to say, as he wraps the book with reflections on how "what we have here is your classic damned-if-you-do-and-damned-if-you-don't." But it is the happiest ending he can offer and it doesn't make him too downhearted. Life goes on, but if "you have to face [life] with more questions than answers, it can be a crying shame."

Bailey's Café teaches people of faith a number of important lessons. In particular, it presents a secular version of the communion of saints. As we already know, "saints" are not just the holy people, but all human beings seeking greater and richer humanity. Everyone who shows up at the café does so out of the need to move in that direction and, perhaps, with some kind of inchoate recognition that this is possible only with the help of others. Sadie, Esther, Peaches, Mariam, and Jesse Bell all succeed to an extent, but only through the interventions of Bailey, Nadine, Eve, and perhaps Gabe. Their success is limited, but it is real, and in these stories we see Bailey's vision of the world, an open-ended struggle for authenticity where pain and suffering are all too apparent. There are those who can recognize their world in the café, the multitudes of human beings of any faith or none who know only too well that beyond the back door lies the abyss, who struggle with poverty, abuse, drugs, and alcohol. And there are those, so many of us, for whom faith is not such a struggle because the world we know is not so fragile. But to know that indeed the world *is* this fragile, and that the way to confront the fragility is together, not alone, is a valuable lesson about where and how we encounter grace. People of faith can read *Bailey's Café* and recall the judgment of the Lord in chapter 25 of Matthew's gospel, where faith in Christ is validated in the corporal works of mercy. To the secular mind, this novel teaches a lesson about the ubiquity of human dignity. No one is so low that a flame of love does not burn somewhere inside. Grace or love, call it what you will, is at work in the café and, indeed, in Eve's "boarding-house."

One of the values of a work of magical realism like *Bailey's Café* is that it signals by its slipperiness that there is something beyond the story that is being told. What is it, exactly, that lies outside the back door? Sometimes it seems simply to be the abyss, at others a medium for joy and gratitude, a place to enter a cosmic dance in which in some strange way love and healing are present. It is both promising and dangerous, or rather it is one or the other depending on the way in which each person embraces the possibility. Out there is an unnamable mystery, the back door to the café is the horizon beyond which lies ultimate mystery, what Henry James indeed calls "the matter." And it is perhaps not altogether too fanciful to invoke the power of the imagination's influence on what different people might encounter outside the rear door. Sadie steps back, perhaps because she knows that her real self is too beclouded with alcohol to make real the fantasy she is indulging about her future life with Iceman Jones. For her, reality defeats the imagination, while Mariam imagines all too strongly and disappears into a world of her own creation.

Good and Evil in Three Pines

One of the ways in which to establish in a nonelitist fashion the category of "serious" fiction is to consider a candidate for inclusion that at first glance would be dismissed as "light." Looking within the genre of detective fiction may seem to some to be a fruitless search, though there is no doubt that over the past thirty years the psychological depth of the work of whodunnits has expanded enormously. The classic detective fiction of the likes of John Dickson Carr or Agatha Christie, of Margery Allingham, Ellery Queen, or Ngaio Marsh, is essentially about puzzle solving. Christie parades a series of stock characters before us and defies us to work out who is the murderer. There is always a vicar, an ex-military man harrumphing his way through the pages, a bluff businessman, and a society woman. The sleuth, be it Hercule Poirot or Miss Marple, solves the puzzle. We never learn anything about either of them; there is no backstory. Nor is there for Allingham's Campion or Sayers's Lord Peter Wimsey or Marsh's Roderick Alleyn. But something did begin to change about thirty years ago.

These days everyone is writing detective fiction, but a few are doing something interesting. The bulk of the output falls into the subgenre of "British cosy" that descends most directly from the classic authors mentioned above, though the location is as likely to be Montana or Shanghai as St. Mary Mead. Most of these, and there are an enormous number, need not detain us. There is nothing wrong with them as entertainments, but few of them mean more than they say. Among their ranks, however, and particularly in the sub-subgenre of "police procedurals" we can single out a few that deserve more consideration. So, the work of Peter Robinson or the late-lamented Reginald Hill provide extensive backstories for their detectives, including unflattering domestic crises that show, indeed, that our heroes have feet of clay. Ian Rankin's Edinburgh-based John Rebus novels perhaps carry this about as far as anyone has in print, though an even better example might be found in the TV series set in northern England, *Happy Valley*, where Sarah Lancashire's portrayal of police sergeant Catherine Cawood shows us an admirable character who is also deeply flawed.

In looking at *Happy Valley* as an example of something deeper than the average, we encounter the intriguing possibility that in some respects the visual arts may have an advantage over literature. The old line "show don't tell" is truly overused but nevertheless points to a possible plus for TV and movies. Even the more complex of recent police procedural novels tend to telling rather than showing. We are led into the backstory, but for the most part led *through* it to the complex of emotions or psychological problems that the author needs us to be aware of to make the story darker or perhaps simply more intricate. But *Happy Valley* or a number of other such productions are made to show things, not to tell them. We see the dysfunctionality of Cawood's relationships, especially with her recovering alcoholic sister. There is simply no space in a TV drama for someone to explain to us what is going on. And if it leaves less room for the imagination because the images are right there in front of our eyes, it almost cannot fall victim to the weakness of fiction that has to explain that Robinson's Banks is responsible for the failure of his marriage, or that

Elizabeth George's Thomas Lynley hasn't been the same since his wife was murdered.

Though there are probably many choices to make, here we will focus on the Three Pines novels written by the Canadian author Louise Penny over the last fifteen years or so. This is not a random selection. One of the characteristics of this collection of about a dozen books is that most of them revolve around a fairly circumscribed set of characters living in an almost fairytale setting. The village of Three Pines, nestling as it does in southern Quebec not far from the Vermont border, is not on any maps. The principal villagers who reappear in the series of novels include a foul-mouthed elderly woman who serves as the fire chief and who just happens to be one of Canada's finest poets, a dysfunctional couple of artists whose stormy marriage is beset with creative rivalry, a very large black woman who runs the village bookstore, and a gay couple whose bistro seems very much to be at the center of village life. The village itself is idyllic, somewhere we would all like to live. It is, indeed, too good to be true. It is hard enough to believe that such a small village could support a bookshop and a bistro, even harder to accept that the bistro is constantly full of villagers spending their money almost daily on a diet of gourmet foods and fine beverages. But as each story opens, death—or more commonly murder—descends upon the community. Real life threatens if it does not entirely shatter the beauty and peace of Three Pines and the commonsense virtues of its inhabitants. Like *Bailey's Café*, these novels are an exercise in magical realism.

When death visits Three Pines, the Sûreté du Quebec descends upon the town, led by Penny's finest creation, Chief Inspector Armand Gamache. Gamache and his wife Reine-Marie are the principal icons of stability amid the turmoil and insecurities of Three Pines, rather like Bailey and Nadine in their café. Their marriage is a model of love and acceptance. But what makes these stories so complex and satisfying is that the mixture of murkiness and virtue that marks the people of Three Pines is matched by the darkness that lies both in Gamache's past and in the complicated make-up of his assistants. Each one has a substantial backstory, and it all adds up to a series in which the village and the intricacies of the lives of police and people alike are far more significant to the reader than the events surrounding each murder. Through the working out of the violent deaths, more and more is revealed about human nature in general and the complexity of this or that individual in particular. There is pain and suffering in each of their lives, but it is for the most part overcome by goodness. If it is hard to accept that anywhere can be as warm and wonderful as the Three Pines community, it is possible to come away with the feeling that good defeats evil in the end.

If Louise Penny's novels are wonderful examples of detective fiction—and they are—what makes them relevant to the argument we have been developing is the movement back and forth between pure magic and intense realism. The grittiness of police procedurals is intertwined with the daily doings of this French Canadian version of Brigadoon or Shangri-La. The town, the stories, and the characters struggle with the mystery of good and evil in all lives and in all places. Uncomplicated people have no place in Three Pines. Gamache's closest assistant, Jean-Guy Beauvoir, comments on his boss: "Gamache was the best of them, the smartest and bravest and strongest because he was willing to go into his own head alone, and open all the doors there, and enter all the dark rooms. And make friends with what he found there."[10]

While there is very little if any overt reference to religion in these novels, without question the idea of redemption is never far from the surface, usually redemption from a past with which one or another has failed thus far to come to terms. And Armand Gamache is the prime example, both a fount of wis-

---

[10] Louise Penny, *A Fatal Grace* (New York: Minotaur Books, 2011).

dom and a wonderful mentor to his underlings, a man of great
humanity and of immense warmth of character, yet damaged
to a degree by the evil that others have done and the mistakes
of his past. The crucial insight, for Gamache and so many others in the series, is that the strength we see in them is a direct
result of the darkness overcome, or at least borne bravely. The
elderly poet Ruth Zardo is a challenging figure. As Olivier, one
of the bistro owners observes, "When Ruth Zardo ordered you
into a conflagration, you went. She was scarier than a burning
building."[11] Scary she is, though with a soft spot for animals,
substituting in mid-series a duck for her beloved dog. In *The
Nature of the Beast* she announces the theme, but it could stand
for any one of the novels: "And now it is now. . . . And the
dark thing is here."[12] But for all the darkness, in the end, good
triumphs. These are crime novels, classically comic rather than
tragic. The tragedy is overcome, happiness returns to the village, often enough tinged with sadness, and the story closes.
But there is always the next one, or so we hope.

Recalling Wolfgang Iser's distinction between attitude and
interpretation, we can perhaps see how the Three Pines novels
break through from the former to the latter category. If we
simply take them as intriguing mysteries with a sense of place
and a cast of extraordinary characters, we will stay on the very
enjoyable surface and we will not gain all that there is to gain.
The telling rather than showing that inevitably preponderates,
as in Beauvoir's estimation of Gamache above, is not in itself
the breakthrough to a text that invites interpretation. But alongside or perhaps beneath this is a different pulse. There is the
deep mystery of human relationships, itself made up of the
deep mystery of individuals, in the marriage of Peter and
Clara, in the humorous and forgiving partnership of Armand
and Reine-Marie, and in the equally interesting gay twosome

[11] Louise Penny, *Still Life* (New York: Minotaur Books, 2008).
[12] Louise Penny, *The Nature of the Beast* (New York: Minotaur Books, 2016).

of Gabri and Olivier. As the series of novels unfolds, two of these couples have enormous challenges to surmount, and in their different ways they eventually succeed, though not without considerable pain. The depiction of what transpires is indeed a matter of showing, not telling. Louise Penny has said that in the end her books are about enduring love. This mystery of grace is not in the telling but in the showing, and it surely explains the enormous outpouring of awards for her twelve novels. The readers come back time and again not so much for the puzzle but more for the characters. And what we find in the characters is a set of lessons about what matters most in life, not in Three Pines so much as wherever we find ourselves.

One of Louise Penny's novels is an outlier in the sense that Three Pines plays no role in it, but it helps us make our point about the series in general. *A Beautiful Mystery*[13] is set in a remote monastery and has three foci: a murder, of course; the beauty and mystery of Gregorian chant; and the complex dynamics between Gamache, Beauvoir, and their superior officer, the sinister and amoral Sylvain Francoeur. We are given insight into the backstory of treachery that meant an end to Gamache's hopes of further promotion and earned him the undying hatred of Francoeur for uncovering corruption at the highest level of the Sûreté. But at the same time we are treading water in our deeper progress into the human condition that the Three Pines stories excel at communicating. This perhaps suggests a way in which what is often considered the more mundane literary form of the detective story can rise above itself. One Three Pines mystery is intriguing, but as the series develops, and the characters along with the stories of murder and mayhem, readers begin to gather insight into the loves and at times hatreds that bind this community together. As Penny put it in the lines at the beginning of this chapter, the fundamental

[13] Louise Penny, *A Beautiful Mystery* (New York: Minotaur Books, 2013).

mystery about which she is writing is that of *enduring* love. And enduring love cannot be told; it must be shown. We have to be allowed to develop at least something of that enduring love that is being explored among the very human characters, people and police alike, who appear over and over again in these stories. It takes ten of the twelve novels for the complex marriage of Peter and Clara to achieve resolution, and it takes just as many for us to come to see that the rude and selfish Ruth Zardo is actually a pearl of great price.

With Louise Penny we return to the theological notion of the communion of saints. The saints on earth, unlike their forerunners among the heavenly host, are the only ones who encounter both the mystery of grace and the allure of sin in daily life. There can be no sin among the blessed and there can be no struggle in the eternal rest that is their reward. Traditionally that part of the communion of saints now alive in the world was described as "the church militant," to distinguish them from the church triumphant in heaven. Usually this militancy was understood to depict the role of struggling against the force of evil in the world, symbolized in the figure of Satan and his demons. If we have moved away from seeing church and world as opposed to one another, we are perhaps enabled better to see that it is in the individual's earthly struggle for integrity that grace and sin are juxtaposed and in the worldly and ecclesial communities that integrity is enabled and supported. So the communion of saints becomes a theological term for the human condition, life on earth lived out in relationship with others, even global solidarity, in which "salvation" may depend not so much on routing the enemy as on the day-to-day intentionality toward the acceptance of grace. Grace, of course, is a synonym for love, but the qualifier "enduring" says a lot about both.

■ ■ ■ ■ ■ ■ *Chapter Nine* ■ ■ ■ ■ ■ ■

Saving Stories

"Faith always sounds like an act of will. Frankly, I don't know what faith in God means. For me, the experience is much more a sense of God. Nothing could be more miraculous than the fact that we have a consciousness that makes the world intelligible to us and are moved by what is beautiful."

(Marilynne Robinson)[1]

All that we have said thus far in these considerations circles around the striking parallels in the *structures* of the act of faith and the act of reading, but there remains a question about how the *content* of the novel pertains to the matter of faith. To answer this question we shall need to delve into the dramatics of plot and the way in which through the imagination the plot of the novel can relate to and inform the dramatics of the reader's own "plot," that is, the narrative of the reader's life as it is unfolding. Reading a novel, we are immersed in a narrative text created by an author, which we encounter at a particular moment in the dynamics of our own lives. What this moment is, what point we are at in our personal story, will be highly relevant to the way we appropriate the meaning of the text.

---

[1] Marilynne Robinson, "The Art of Fiction No. 198," interviewed by Sarah Fay, *The Paris Review* 186 (Fall 2008); http://www.theparisreview.org/interviews/5863/the-art-of-fiction-no-198-marilynne-robinson.

When we return to the childhood books we loved, how different they may seem to us, perhaps deeper or perhaps less significant, because where we are now in every respect is different from where we were then. Read a great book in tandem with a close friend with whom you share a lot, and marvel at the different nuances, and maybe more, that each of you has seen in the same text. Gender, age, and life circumstance may also influence these differences. How different indeed must it be for the same person to read Tolstoy's *The Death of Ivan Ilyich* as a healthy college undergraduate, as a too-busy middle-manager struggling for preferment in the corporate rat race, and as someone in the prime of life suddenly confronted with terminal illness. A veteran of active military duty will surely see much more in Tolkien's *The Lord of the Rings* than the young boy who is excited by the story and sets out to learn Elvish. And would it be wrong to suggest that Toni Morrison's *Beloved* inevitably speaks differently to the descendants of slaves than it does to white Americans, and differently to them than, say, Latvians or Swedes?

For all the variations that we can imagine among readers encountering the same text, and for all that all readers reading many different texts imbibe, at the same time something similar is going on, whether twelve-year-old Jenny is exploring *Little Women* or her twin brother cannot get enough of *The Chronicles of Narnia* or their mother just put down *Mrs. Dalloway* with a deep sigh of satisfaction or Dad is doggedly working his way through some of the murkier Faulkners. Thus far, we have described this common something quite formally as the creation of the aesthetic object in the space between text and reader, where the imagination is hard at work though at best only glimpsing "the matter" that is the deepest level of truth, so deep that not even the author is fully aware of it (remember Henry James?). Depicting the act of reading in this way it has been relatively easy to suggest a parallel to how the mystery of God is related to the act of faith of a believing individual, always somehow there, always veiled, always impossible to grasp fully. So much for structural similarities. But now we need to explore the two, faith and fiction, more substantively. What about the content of the novel and the content of the act of faith? Is it possible that they may even be closer to one another than we have imagined in our discussion of structural parallels?

When we begin to think about the substance of the act of faith, we must disabuse ourselves of any notion that "God" is its content. God is not the content of the act of faith; God, in fact, is the other of the act of faith. The content is something that in principle we can grasp fully, in this case the dynamics of faith as they unfold in each of our lives, as we orient ourselves in love toward an other, God, whom we cannot fully comprehend. The content of faith is our own faith story, the dynamic interaction of our searching after love and our being found by love and the lifelong challenge of maintaining and deepening that love in the face of all that may cheapen, weaken, or even destroy it. In the content of faith, the other of faith draws near to us, though we may be unable to name the mystery, but the starting and perhaps the ending point is found in faithfulness to the content, to the growth in the capacity to give and receive love. As the first letter of John puts it so well, "whoever does not love their brother and sister, whom they have seen, cannot love God, whom they have not seen" (1 John 4:20). This is also the message of the famous last judgment scene in Matthew 25. When the Lord distinguishes between the sheep and the unfortunate goats it is not on the grounds that they have been able to name or recognize the Lord but that they have reached out in love to the needy around them. When they have done this, then they have encountered the Lord, though perhaps they could not have named him. And in what is surely an anticipation of this great drama, Jesus in the same gospel warns that "not everyone who says to me, 'Lord, Lord,' will enter the kingdom of heaven, but only the one who does the will of my Father who is in heaven" (7:21). The will of the Father is spelled out in chapter 25. And the conclusion must surely be that the act of faith, understood as fidelity to the giving and receiving of love, is not necessarily connected to any explicit naming of an object of faith. It is quite possible, in fact, that a life lived in commitment to the giving and receiving of love in the absence of any formal religious convictions points even more clearly to the end point of Christian mysticism, that "God is love," than do all the wordy outpourings of organized religion.

When we suggest that the act of faith is rightly described as the lifelong deepening of the capacity to give and receive love, and hence largely to erase any difference between how that plays out in the life of someone with formal religious convictions and someone without them, we understand the growth and maturation of a human being to be directly related to growth toward God. Growth in love, growth toward God, and growth in human flourishing are all different ways of describing much the same process.[2] There are, of course, differences between the ways in which more religious and more secular individuals will describe this process. A Christian will express growing self-coherence as growing toward God or growing closer to Jesus Christ and may indeed monitor the character of "true love" by turning to the gospels or seeking guidance in prayer. Someone who does not share this faith will have other ways to describe the growth of love and the potential for its taking wrong paths, of becoming less true (which a Christian might call "sinful"), but what seems to be beyond doubt is that the narrative of both Judaism and Christianity represents God willing to create human beings in the divine image

---

[2] This is Karl Rahner's idea of self-coherence, discussed at some length in chap. 7 above. Rahner's discussion can be found in his essay "Current Problems in Christology," in *Theological Investigations* 1 (Baltimore, MD: Helicon, 1965), 149–200, esp. 162.

204 The Wounded Angel

and likeness, without distinctions of gender, race, or anything else. When Adam and Eve are expelled from the Garden of Eden their relationship to God does not come to an end, and they are still made in the divine image and likeness. Their new task in their sinful condition is not to find God again but through human love to let God find them. In the Christian trinitarian understanding of God, God as Spirit inhabits human love (this is the mystery of grace once again) and enfolds that love back into the life of God. Where we see human love, we see the process of divinization at work.

The depiction of a human life as a movement toward an ever-deepening capacity to love and be loved is at the most profound level what is meant by the notion of salvation. Obviously, to think in this way about salvation requires us to step away from more popular notions that it is somehow a reward for a life of religious fidelity, even less that it is something we can attain through the performance of certain practices and obedience to certain commands. These traditional ways of thinking about salvation are on the right track in that they are imagining divine grace as the sanctifier but erroneous in conceiving of this grace as a something bestowed from on high as a reward for this or that. Divine grace is inside us from the first moment of our existence, inseparable from our nature as created in the divine image. The more we live lives of deep humanity and humaneness, the more we love and receive love, the more we are conformed to the divine image and likeness. "Salvation" hints etymologically at the idea of healing and at that of being rescued. The former connotation makes it much easier to see how being a person of faith or not is not directly connected to the possibility of salvation. The more fully we become who we are the more closely we are conformed to the divine image and likeness. God's will that human beings grow closer to God by growing in love can only be frustrated by human willfulness. Our condition in life, our faith or lack of it, are immaterial to our capacity to love. Salvation is living in love, which in itself is conforming us to our eternal destiny in God. "Not everyone who says to me, 'Lord, Lord,' will enter the kingdom of heaven, but only the one who does the will of my Father who is in heaven."

Just as the understanding of salvation has to grow and change in this way of thinking, so what we mean by "growing in love and in the capacity to be loved" needs to be understood in a more nuanced and complex fashion than popular conceptions of love would settle for. Love and desire are somehow inseparable, but the healthy desire is that which desires the good of the other, and our own good only insofar as it aids the good of the other. The other here can of course be a single individual with whom we are in love, but its richest expression is in willing and loving the good of the world, of the gift of life itself, in the end, of all living things. All the great spiritual writers agree in valuing this kind of self-giving love as the highest form of love, not least because in the practice of self-giving we become more and more fully ourselves. So many of Jesus' best-known words insist on as much.

There are two important respects in which this theological understanding of salvation is connected to the relationship between faith and fiction. For the person of faith serious literature is a window on the complexities of human loving, the challenges it faces, and the danger of easy dismissal of what does not seem to fit the notions of love that we may have imbibed through the doctrinal teachings of our own tradition. Reading literature broadens the religious mind and destroys easy polarities. But much more important, it offers countless versions of what the religious imagination will see as stories of what we can call the coming-to-be of salvation. And for the secular imagination unencumbered by doctrine, great literature is a kind of schooling in the centrality of loving and being loved in the task of human living. This reader traverses the same path as the person of faith, even if the categories of sin and grace are alien to secular understanding. It does not matter so much if the novel is comic or tragic, so long as its message is not that of simple despair or sheer frivolity. When the secular imagination learns through great literature to explore more deeply the connection between love and human depth, the reader is brought into the place of being saved. And while the person of faith will name the role of God in grounding this mystery, the nonbeliever cannot but be faced with the question of whether or not the love/humanity connection does not lift at least a corner of the veil that hides the answer to the quintessentially fundamental question of the meaning of the whole. The person of faith does not have all the answers, though she or he may have words to name what is happening, and the nonbeliever is not bereft of the opportunity to sense that there is more going on here than we can easily explain.

For both the religious and the secular person, it is the imagination that is key. As Coleridge would put it, it is in our encounter with the creative artist's capacity to employ the secondary imagination that our own imaginations can glimpse the primary imagination that lies beyond anyone's grasp. When we love a book we may be grateful to the author and we may be attracted to or repelled by the characters, but it is the way that we have imaginatively responded to the whole on which we base our judgment of its significance. How has the way the story is told worked upon our imaginations? How have we been able to appropriate the depths of what has occurred? How, in the end, does the plot of this fiction speak to and enlarge my sense of the plot of my own life? Or in the words we have been using thus far in this chapter, how does the fiction's depiction of the becoming of love speak to the dynamics of love in the reader's own life? I can make it my own only through the work of my imagination. In the power of great fiction lies the capacity to enliven and enrich the workings of the human imagination, religious or secular.

If we grant that reading fiction of substance somehow enriches our humanity and deepens our appreciation for life, and if we are ready to accept that in our growing self-coherence we are, whether we know it or not, opening ourselves to divine grace, then we can surely see that great stories are salvific. They do not transform us overnight from one kind of person to another. They do not "save" in this sense. Salvation, like the reign of God in Jesus's preaching, is already with and within us. To embrace this reality is the gift of faith, but to live within its truth is God's gift to humanity, given with our creation in the divine image and likeness. Stories in the hands of great artists open windows to possibility. They show us how God is at work in human loving and being loved, and they warn us of the resistance that human beings show all too often to the call to love and be loved generously and without reserve. Where there is grace in our lives, there is also going to be sin; where there is love, there is also the danger of self-idolatry and the enticements of ersatz versions of love. We cannot all of us all of the time be aware of how fiction is an instrument of divine pedagogy, but consciously sometimes and at others subliminally, our selves are slowly refashioned by the stories of sin and grace that we read. If we come away from *The Brothers Karamazov* or *The Grapes of Wrath* unchanged, then perhaps we have not given our imaginations room to roam. We haven't really been reading.

While the grace of God is by no means present only in serious fiction, there is an important way in which its particular presence in fiction works on its readers. Great art and music, poetry, the "aha" moment in scientific inquiry, and the quietude of contemplation all offer access to the love of God, perhaps in ways that prose literature cannot achieve. They may free the imagination entirely of the inevitable constraints to its exercise that come with entering into a narrative. Think about what we have seen possible in the painting of *The Wounded Angel*. But because story is a narrative and salvation is a word for living life in the grace of God, the fact that fiction has a plot while art and music and most poetry do not makes it especially nutritious for reflection on the plot of our own lives. Our "plots" are lifelong narratives of sin and grace. The dramatic tension in each of our lives is provided by the impact of external circumstances and other human beings on the purity of our need to love and be loved. Fictions supply us with an abundance of examples of how others negotiate this tension. The characters may be imaginary, but the plots are real instances of the tensions of sin and grace that abound in all lives, including our own. I may not decide to act like Alyosha Karamazov or Emma Woodhouse, but from the writings of Fyodor Dostoevsky and Jane Austen I can learn a great deal about the mysteries of love and grace.

In the novel, and to a lesser extent in the short story, the plots of our own lives as sites of sin and grace are brought into relationship with the story laid out for us by the imagination of the author. The nourishing of our ongoing condition of being saved is not given to us by the author or even by the text but, as we have seen already so often, by the work of our imaginations as we build what Wolfgang Iser called "the aesthetic object." The author in all probability is not consciously interested in the notion of salvation, and the text is equally unlikely to be using the categories of sin and grace, though it will inevitably be taken up with this tension, however it is named. (Reread Henry James's masterpiece, *Portrait of a Lady*, and tell me that this most secular of authors is not immersed in matters of sin, grace, and salvation.) So in the space between the text and the reader, where each reader creates a personal aesthetic object by reading the text as someone whose life is its own narrative of the mixed fortunes of loving and being loved, the reader's ongoing salvation is being nourished and deepened. This is where James Wood is both correct and incorrect when he writes that "fiction moves in the shadow of doubt, knows itself to be a true lie, knows that at any moment it might fail to make its case." "Being the game of not-quite," he continues, fiction "is the place of not-quite belief."[3] Fiction is surely a fabrication, in the sense of something made, but this is not the same as a lie. Unless perhaps "a true lie" is a way of referring to its mythical character. A myth, after all, is nothing but a fiction that tells truths. Wood's conclusion that "what is a danger in religion is the very fabric of fiction," is more apt. In religion, we both believe in and believe the voice of the holy. We may believe in fiction, in its power to address and challenge us, but we believe it only provisionally, since it is a fabrication (if not a lie). Religious faith, however, cannot be possessed provisionally.

Someone possessed of Christian faith is in a distinctly different position from those of other faiths or none, because the Christian's imagination is shaped by two stories, that of creation and that of the incarnation, death, and resurrection of Jesus Christ. It is not that the Christian brings preconceptions of good and evil or sin and grace to reading fiction. Openness to the text is essential, whether the reader is or is not a person of religious faith. But the life that the Christian brings to the text is already shaped in a certain way, and to some degree all Christians' lives are shaped similarly. This means only that what Christians bring to the mysterious fashioning of the aesthetic object, like any other reader, is influenced by who they are. The mystery beyond the horizon of the text, what Henry James called "the matter," will be identified with the Christian mystery of the incomprehensible love of God. The reader who does not possess the plot that the Christian is given in the tradition will be reading with the same attention and engaged in the same imaginative work of fashioning the aesthetic object, but without the intention or even perhaps the capacity to name it in the way that religious faith makes possible. On the other hand, the easier openness to what the text has to offer that

---

[3] James Wood, *The Broken Estate: Essays on Literature and Belief* (New York: Picador, 1999, 2010), xx–xxi.

comes with the absence of faith-inspired presuppositions makes it less likely that the secular reader will distort or mishear the message of the text. The Christian has to be much more attentive to the dangers of eisegesis and open to the possibility that the most cherished notions about the mystery of God may be challenged in the aesthetic object that is created by imaginative interaction with the text.

If there is one preeminent indicator that an individual is on the right path, it is surely that we can say that he or she is a happy person. This happiness does not, however, come from the fulfillment of desires or the satisfaction of needs, real or imagined, but rather from a life shaped by contented commitment to a particular task, where "happiness" really means human flourishing. Hedonistic pleasures come and go, but our enduring satisfaction must be based on the conviction that for all our faults we have lived our lives in a consistent effort to become more and more who we are meant to be. As Aristotle puts it, "the function of man is to live a certain kind of life, and this activity implies a rational principle, and the function of a good man is the good and noble performance of these, and if any action is well performed it is performed in accord with the appropriate excellence: if this is the case, then happiness turns out to be an activity of the soul in accordance with virtue."[4] This kind of happiness is the only lasting kind, the kind that comes with consistency between who we are and what we do. At one and the same time, this understanding corrects religious narrowness of vision and failings of imagination, and expands the imagination's appreciation of the actual closeness between what people of faith might refer to as moments of grace and what a more secular gaze might prefer to call an appreciation for life.

To illustrate more concretely this set of somewhat abstract reflections, let us see how they work out in practice in three

---

[4] Aristotle, *Nicomachean Ethics* (London: Penguin, 2004), 1098a13.

types of novels, each of which is differently connected to explicitly religious faith. There are first those that are framed in distinctly religious terms, and Marilynne Robinson's novel *Gilead*,[5] which begins and ends within a Christian religious worldview and something of a Calvinist theological outlook, can serve here as the epitome. A second group is consciously oriented toward mystery but without any explicitly religious framework. David James Duncan's *The River Why*,[6] the story of the spiritual awakening of the young Gus Orviston, in which fishing for salmon and steelhead is a way of encountering the holy, can stand as an exemplar of this second type. Finally, there are those novels in which the categories of sin and grace, if addressed at all, are not given overtly spiritual significance, and C. E. Morgan's two books, *All the Living*[7] and *The Sport of Kings*,[8] are fine instances of this more secular approach. What is it in each of these three kinds of texts that orients and corrects all readers of whatever set of beliefs to the place of mystery in the aesthetic object they are fashioning? It will be our contention that the awareness of grace, however it is named, is what moves the imagination in that direction.

Gilead

Marilynne Robinson distinguishes between "mercy, which is given in despite of faults, and grace, for whom no fault exists."[9] This slightly gnomic utterance is intended to stress the gratuitousness of grace, that it is blind to the question of merit, while divine mercy is extended to those whose sinfulness requires it. Unlike more secular readers, Christians will

[5] Marilynne Robinson, *Gilead* (New York: Farrar, Strauss, Giroux, 2004).

[6] David James Duncan, *The River Why* (Boston, MA: Back Bay Books, 2016).

[7] C. E. Morgan, *All the Living* (New York: Picador, 2010).

[8] C. E. Morgan, *The Sport of Kings* (New York: Farrar, Strauss, Giroux, 2016).

[9] Marilynne Robinson, *The Givenness of Things* (New York: Farrar, Strauss and Giroux, 2015), 223.

understand both mercy and grace as emanating from God. Since human beings are not in the judgment business (unless they want to be judged themselves), mercy is God's to dispense. There is, of course, a form of human mercy that can either be the virtue of forgiveness or the staying of the axe that constitutes "showing mercy," and this may be the only sense in which it can be understood by those for whom the category of divine mercy is not helpful. "Grace" is not susceptible to the same variations, however. Grace is God's alone; it is the love of God active in the world, and not a notion that works easily without a sense of a divine dispenser, though the words "graciousness" and "graceful" carry with them into our secular age the remnants of the religious sense they once exclusively possessed. Indeed, divine mercy is nothing other than an instance of grace, in this case the love of God in the form of forgiveness. We are all fallible, all sinners, and we deserve judgment, but in God's grace we receive mercy instead. As Robinson suggested in the essay just quoted, grace is different because it is bestowed freely without any sense of need or merit. It is a free gift.

Gilead is the life story of the Iowa preacher John Ames, told by him in the form of a letter to his young son, to be read only when the seven-year-old reaches adulthood. With the exception of two years in seminary, Ames has lived his entire life in Gilead, half a century of it serving as pastor to the little faith community. His first wife died in childbirth many years before, and his second marriage surprised him in his late sixties. Now seventy-six, with a young son, he sets out to explain himself ostensibly to the adult son that will one day be, but perhaps in reality to himself. As a good Calvinist he is not unaware of his own failings before God, but even more aware of the outpourings of God's grace in his life. Surprisingly, perhaps, the signs of his good fortune consist mostly of human love, whether that of his two wives or his son, or of Boughton, his lifelong friend and fellow pastor. In Robinson's skillful hands the focus is on how satisfied Ames is with the way his life has unfolded, even though much of it has been anything but pleasurable. Ames lost his first wife in childbirth, and the child shortly after. He then lived alone for forty years in the small Iowa community. Looking back further he recounts the difficult relationships between his fiery, gun-toting pastor grandfather and his pacifist pastor father. And even as he thinks of his second wife, much younger than him, and their very young son, the genuine pleasure he feels in their love for one another is tinged with the sadness that comes from knowing his life is nearing its end. His biggest challenge, however, seems to come from the return to Gilead of John Ames Boughton, the ne'er-do-well son of "old" Robert Boughton, his pastor friend. Ames deeply distrusts Jack, as he is known, and does not like the friendly relationship be strikes up with Ames's young son. Even here, though, as the tale unfolds it becomes clear that Jack is graced, for all his sinfulness, and that Ames's judgment on him may be in some measure a failing. All in all, Ames sees his life as having been one of quiet satisfaction, not complacency so much as the assurance of the fittingness of all that has transpired in his life, even the painful losses he would undo if he could. His life illustrates what Robinson might call "the givenness of things," a phrase she uses as the title of her most recent book of essays.[10]

All readers of whatever religious persuasion have much to learn from the way in which Ames appreciates the shape of his life, now that near the end he can see it more clearly. If we are able to step back from narrowly religious categories like salvation and providence, we might see that what is most evident in *Gilead* is how what happens in our lives, however we might express it, is an instance of "the givenness of things." We do not control what happens in our lives, however much we may try. Some things come to us and some do not, of

[10] See the previous note.

course, and some are things we want but cannot have, and some are things we don't want but find ourselves saddled with. But the individual thing is not quite the point. Rather, it is that our whole lives in all their complexity come to us as unmerited and unconstrained. We do not earn what happens to us, and we are not bound by it. The happy person receives what life gives, good and bad alike, and works on it to fashion an existence that is coherent. Each of us, if we would be happy, is the result of our free and creative acceptance of all that is given to us.

Reading *Gilead* is therapy for both the religious and—perhaps more surprising—the secular imagination. As we have noted previously, the religious imagination in our own day tends to be mired in prodigiously prosaic categories. Step aside for a moment from the ethical categories that seem so often to be what religious people and their parent traditions mistake for piety. What remains is so often a matter of routinized ritual, as if church were a kind of gymnasium for the soul. What all the founders of the world's religious traditions have taught is in one form or another the embrace of the joys and pains of life, and Ames is someone who has learned this wisdom as he has aged. If we look at even a few of the passages in which Ames sees graced moments, they are evidently graced because they are so intensely human. He is happiest when he sees his son and wife "making sandwiches with peanut butter and apple butter on raisin bread,"[11] or when "they were playing a waltz on the radio" and deciding to dance to it; he remembers his youthful athleticism playing catch and concludes, "Oh, I will miss the world."[12] Recounting his courtship of his second wife, he comments on the softness of her voice: "That there should be such a voice in the whole world, and that I should be the one to hear it, seemed to me then and seems to me now

[11] Robinson, *Gilead*, 117.
[12] Ibid., 115.

an unfathomable grace."[13] Closing the journal, he mentions "prevenient" grace, the grace "that precedes grace itself and allows us to accept it," but chastises himself because "that is the pulpit speaking." His final words to his son are simpler, "I'll pray that you grow up a brave man in a brave country. I will pray that you find a way to be useful."[14]

Fishing for Happiness

David James Duncan's novel *The River Why*[15] is a coming-of-age story and therefore well suited to our focus in this final chapter on plot. It is also an immensely funny book, which places it in a somewhat different category from most of the novels with which we have been spending time. *Gilead* has some very amusing moments, but *The River Why* is simply zany, especially in the early chapters. At the same time it is deeply thoughtful, even mystical, in its appropriation of the wisdom of all traditions, religious or not, in the search for the key to happiness. It is apparent from the outset that the answer is somehow connected to fishing, but it takes Gus Orviston, the hero and narrator of the story, until almost the end of this lengthy book to figure it out.

Gus and his parents, whom he calls Ma and H20, are utterly obsessed with fishing but mostly unable to agree with one another. H20 only recognizes the value of fly-fishing, while Ma is equally committed to bait-fishing, and arguments erupt daily between the wisecracking and tough talking mother and her uptight and ever-so-well-educated husband. They are an odd couple to say the least, as if Ma Kettle had married William F. Buckley. There is also a younger son, a slightly

[13] Ibid., 209.

[14] Ibid., 246–47.

[15] *The River Why* was first published by Sierra Club Books in 1983 and was reissued by Back Bay Books with an afterword by the author in 2016.

autistic *Wunderkind* named Bill Bob, who is not the least bit interested in fishing and who lives in his own private world, with two transistor radios (this is the 1960s) strapped to his head. As the story unfolds Gus meets many unique individuals, philosophers and fishing people alike, a number of children, a dog called Descartes who speaks wisdom, though only through the mouth of his owner, and—most important— the beautiful Eddy, a young woman with whom Gus becomes romantically entangled, partially for her beauty and at least as much for her fishing skills.

For most of the story Gus has been freeing himself from his totally compulsive approach to fishing, though not from the fishing itself. Early on in the story Gus leaves home and goes off into the woods to live alone in a cabin and to concentrate on fishing. He creates a ridiculous "ideal schedule" in which he carves out for himself fourteen and a half hours of fishing a day. In time this proves unsustainable and unsatisfying and he moderates his passion, mixing it up with study and a more balanced social life. But it is only when he and Eddy fall in love that the full truth of things is made apparent to Gus. After a first, passionate week together in his forest cabin, Eddy tells him that she will be leaving for twenty-four hours and assigns him a task to fill the time she will be away. As evening falls she loads his pockets with food and water and takes him down to the river. Then she casts a very fine fishing line and successfully hooks a large salmon. Handing the line to him, she tells him to play the fish. If you fight it, the line will break, she says, and leaves. Gus slowly realizes that his purpose is not to catch the fish so much as to set it free. Through the night he follows it as it swims upstream, heading to the point where it (now revealed as a she) will deposit its eggs to be fertilized by its mate, and then the two of them will die, leaving the eggs to hatch in the following spring. As the night goes on, Gus and the fish travel miles together, never straining the line to the point of breaking. So long as the line is not taut, the fish is free to swim, but it remains literally attached to Gus. And then, as in some mysterious way the trust between man and fish has developed, Gus is able to reach out, touch the salmon, and release her from the line.

In this deeply spiritual and religiously pluralistic but theologically undogmatic novel Gus is led by the experience with the fish to a kind of mystical vision, a vision of a "vertical bar" linking the earth "to a realm that light alone could enter." Falling to his knees, he feels a hand on his head and he "knew that the line of light led not to a realm but to a Being, and that the light and the hook were his, and that they were made of love alone."[16] In the end, Gus and Eddy are married, Bill Bob takes up fishing, and Ma and H20 switch their preferred forms of fishing and cement their newly restored harmony by producing a baby sister for Gus and Bill Bob. But if it is love that is celebrated in the end here, it is the love to which Gus has found his way, the love that ceases to struggle with or against the object of love, to let the loved one be simply who she or he is, to the insight that the happiness of the lover comes from promoting the happiness of the loved one. Gus, like John Ames, has learned that love is not about hunt and capture.

Several strands in the concluding pages of *The River Why* save it from the formulaic pieties that one might imagine it proclaims from the brief summary of the story offered here. First of all, the fish are respected and freed for the most part, but sometimes—respectfully too—they are killed and eaten, in the way in which the Native Americans of the plains understood their relationship to the buffalo. Second, Duncan prefaces the final chapter of the book, the one in which all the loose ends are tied up in a way that would do justice to any Shakespearian comedy, with stern words of Meister Eckhart: "God lies in wait for us with nothing so much as love, and love is like a fisherman's hook. . . . He who is caught by it is held by

---

[16] Duncan, *The River Why*, 383.

the strongest of bonds, and yet the stress is pleasant. . . . Moreover, he can sweetly bear all that happens to him; all that God inflicts he can take cheerfully." "Whatever he does," ends the quotation from Eckhart, "who is caught by this hook, love does it, and love alone."[17] Third and last, Gus recounts the story of Master Hu, an old Taoist in ancient China. Hu has a robust relationship with God, and the principal sign of their friendship is that Hu calls God names and God afflicts Hu with sores, arthritis, gout, and so on. The people cannot understand this, but ugly old Hu is not fazed, because he loves God and knows that God loves him. And then one day, "God took his line in hand and drew him right into Himself. That was fine with Hu. That's what a Friend is for."[18]

Though *The River Why* is not a Christian book, it is easy to imagine John Ames nodding his head in affirmation as Gus grows in wisdom and love. And like Ames, Gus arrives at this point through developing a sane way of feeling his oneness with the natural world and a strong sense that he is in the right place, finally, in fishing, family, and love. The ethic here is eudaemonist, not hedonistic. Gus learns that happiness lies in letting go. Of course, he is still a young man and who knows what the future holds for him, though Duncan suggests he will cope by having Bill Bob quote Dame Julian of Norwich in the concluding pages, relating the message God had given her that "all will be well and all manner of things will be well." But there is a level of darkness in this story that *Gilead* does not contain, in the frequent references to human depredation of the natural world, to pollution and exploitation. It is symbolized for Gus in the damage to fish and fishing, and he goes to considerable lengths to rescue one fish trapped in a polluted stream and to set it free in cleaner waters. The larger concern for potential environmental collapse, however, remains. And

[17] Ibid., 386.
[18] Ibid., 402.

the implication is that our freedom and that of the natural world are somehow bound together.

Obsessions

It is perhaps surprising that when we look for a modern novel that is so dark that we must struggle to find the grace in it, we should turn to one written by a young Kentuckian author, C. E. Morgan, who holds a master of divinity degree from Harvard Divinity School. Ostensibly about horse racing, *The Sport of Kings* uses this quintessentially Kentuckian activity to explore much weightier forms of obsession. It is about racing, but it is also about race, and above all it is about obsession with breeding. A championship racehorse is a triumph of breeding, but Morgan's novel shows not only the deeply unpleasant aspects of raising thoroughbred horses but, more important, the corrosive effects of the obsession with success that owners and trainers alike must have if they are to succeed. Breeding a championship racehorse is hedonism at its most striking. Spanning several decades in the mid-twentieth century, the story is bookended by two interracial affairs. In one, the black servant who is discovered to be having a sexual relationship with the white lady of the house is violently disposed of by the master of the house, John Henry Forge. In the latter part of the book, his granddaughter Henrietta Forge becomes passionately involved with a mixed-race man of far humbler origins, Allmon Shaugnessy, with results that are quite different but equally traumatic. At the heart of it all is an obsession with blood and breeding, that requires inbreeding among horses and that spills over into incest in the tragic central figure of the tale, Henrietta's father, Henry Forge. And yet the story ends with a child of mixed blood screaming with delight as the beautiful filly, Hellsmouth, escapes the fire that is destroying Henry Forge's world and with the ghostly return of Allmon to his mother's arms, whom he imagines waiting for him on the other side of the river that separates north and south.

The Sport of Kings flirts with the mystery of grace in the story of Allmon's childhood in Cincinnati with a single mother who struggles to do the best for him and the wisdom of the marvelous figure of his preacher grandfather, just known as "The Reverend." *All the Living* suggests another and ultimately more satisfying way to happiness. This earlier novel is a simpler tale of how human flourishing may depend on a careful balance of contentment and desire. The central character, Aloma, is a young musician who is living on a poor tobacco farm in the middle of nowhere with her lover, Orren, who inherited the farm when his parents died. The central question in the story is whether she will decide to stay or leave, and the temptation to move on comes from a growing friendship with another preacher, Bell Johnson, who initially hires her to play for the Sunday services. When he discovers she is not married to the man with whom she is living, he calls her foolish and ungodly and, in words that hint of his own growing feelings toward her, adds, "Maybe you think it's some small thing to stir up love, but you're wrong."[19] In the final pages, Bell conducts a marriage ceremony for Aloma and Orren, and on the return home to the farm she admits to Orren that she had thought that she had feelings for Bell. Not a great way to begin your married life, but what she seems to see in the end is that she and Orren will sometimes fight and will not always be happy. She can now recognize that Orren needs to work the farm he has inherited, that it is the way in which he can flourish. She, for her part, has earned enough money to rent a piano and plans to give lessons at the farmhouse. In their different ways, they confirm their two selves in what nourishes them most. In a closing moment that cements her identification with *his* need of this place, she takes him to see where his parents thirty

---

[19] Morgan, *All the Living*, 172.

years before had carved their names on a tree. Showing him the carving in the tree that he had never before seen, she simultaneously affirms his way of flourishing and puts her own very different virtuous practice into relationship with his. "Then he took her hand and led her back out of the woods, across the pasture, and up to the old house."[20]

Coda: Form and Substance

Whether we are people of religious faith or not, those of us who read serious fiction certainly do so in part for the pure entertainment value. And yet what distinguishes "serious" fiction from its lighter variants is that there is something beyond the entertainment. Serious fiction is not light reading, for the simple reason that the pleasure and benefits we get from it are in large part due to our willingness to be affected by the something more that is not simply entertainment. Speed reading *Middlemarch* would be a huge mistake; rushing through *The Golden Bowl* would be the height of folly. Aside from the sheer loss of enjoyment that comes from focusing on the events and characters that make up the story and overlooking the telling of the story, the imagination does not come into play when we don't take the time. It is the use of our imaginations that brings us into a creative relationship with the text, without which it washes over like so many thrillers, westerns, crime novels, and even romances. When one of these escapes the confines of its form, as we saw earlier in the case of the work of Louise Penny, it does so because there is something more beyond the plot itself, in her case the development of a cast of characters and a location for most of the events that capture our imagination and lead us inside the stories, resonating and sympathizing with their world, above all, with Armand

[20] Ibid., 199.

Gamache's calm awareness of the pure evil that lurks below the surface of the stories.

The close relationships that we have outlined between the act of reading and the act of faith, and between the plots of our own lives and those we encounter in the fictions, serve to deepen and complicate the creative imagination of all careful readers of any faith and none. To return to a distinction we addressed earlier in our consideration of Coleridge, we are all of us capable of mere fancy, of letting our minds play with this or that feature of a story, or of putting ourselves in the place of one character or another. What is sadly missing in our own day is the sensibility that will reach beyond fancy and be alert to the intimations of deeper mystery and of a sense of the meaning of the whole that all serious fiction of any quality has the power to suggest. It is within our power to rekindle this ability, and in all likelihood for most of us that will happen, if at all, through careful attention to what causes us to wonder— serious fiction, the mysteries of science, the arts in general, contemplation of the natural beauty of the universe. The choice here to focus on fiction is because it is so accessible to us, because it rewards slow and careful consideration (which is itself something our world today is sorely lacking), and because it approaches the mystery of the meaning of the whole, the mystery of the holy (here is the form of fiction) through engaging us in the power of story (here is the substance).

Returning one final time to the image of the wounded angel, we can notice that the angel and the boys carrying the stretcher are on the way somewhere. The angel is on the way to a place of healing, while the boys' souls are nourished by the corporal work of mercy in which they are engaged. Perhaps to them it is just a job, but one that will somehow make them into better people. And perhaps the boy who stares at us so seriously is willing us to stop just looking and enter into the mystery that is being enacted in the picture. Where exactly they are going and what happened to create this tableau is beyond our knowledge; it is part of the mystery. We viewers will never come up with *the* answer to the meaning of the painting. But the mystery of the meaning of the whole, or the mystery of faith in the holy, is something that will nourish our imaginations—can we say our souls?—the more we give ourselves to the works of art of which this painting is just one remarkable example.

Index of Names